G000255894

MEDITERRANEO EDITIONS

Rethymnon
the soul of Crete

Texts:
Stella Kalogeraki
archaeologist

Layout:
Vangelis Papiomytoglou

Fotos:
Vangelis Papiomytoglou

Translation in English:
Alphabet Ltd.

copyright 2006:
MEDITERRANEO EDITIONS
tel: +30 28310 21590, fax: +30 28310 21591,
e-mail: info@mediterraneo.gr

www.mediterraneo.gr

ISBN: 960-8227-12-7

Rethymnon

the soul of Crete

ACQUAINTANCE WITH NATURE 9-33

NATURAL GEOGRAPHY - CLIMATE 10

FLORA 12

THE OLIVE TREE 16

FAUNA 18

CAVES 20

GORGES 24

AREAS OF NATURAL BEAUTY 29

BEACHES 31

3500 YEARS OF CIVILIZATION 35-51

MYTHOLOGY 36

HISTORY 38

Ancient Rithymna
Byzantine Period and Venetian Occupation
The destruction in the year 1571 and the Cretan Renaissance
The siege of Rethymno
From the Turkish Occupation to Autonomy (1669 - 1897)
Autonomy - Union - Modern Times

ARCHAEOLOGICAL SITES 52

Eleftherna
Late Minoan Cemetery of Armeni
Lappa
Syvritos
Axos
Apodoulou
Monasteraki
Stavromenos
Ideon Andron

CHURCHES 61

CONTENTS

MONASTERIES 66

Moni Arkadiou
Moni Preveli
Moni Arsaniou
Moni Atalis / Bali
Moni Aghias Irinis
Moni Chalevi
Moni Vossakou
Moni Diskouriou
Moni Kaloeidenas
Moni Prophet Elias
Moni Antifonitiras in
Myriokefala

VENETIAN MONUMENTS 72

The fortification of the town of
Rethymno
Public Buildings
Private Buildings

MUSEUMS 84

Archaeological Museum of Rethymno
Municipal Gallery "L.Kanakakis"
Historisches Historical and Folklore
Museum
Other museums in Rethymno

FESTIVAL 88

FEASTS AND TRADITIONS 93-105

Religious Holidays
Agricultural Holidays
The Cretan costume
Music and Dances
Handicraft
Dyeing the Fabric
Diet

ITINERARIES 107-135

Tours in Town
Explorng the Prefecture
Foot & bike routes
On the E4 Path

Crete, covering an area of 8,335 Km2 and with a coastline of more than 1000 Km, is the southernmost part of Greece and of the European Union too. It is the largest island in Greece and one of the largest in the Mediterranean. To the north lies the Cretan Sea and to the south the Libyan. Three large mountains dominate the hinterland of the island. To the west are the White Mountains (Lefka Ori) at an altitude of 2,452 m, in the centre, Ida, Psiloritis to the Cretans, the mountain of Zeus at an altitude of 2,456 m and to the east the Dikti range at an altitude of 2,148 m. Crete with a population of around 550,000 has been divided into four provinces since the time of Venetian occupation; Hania in the west, Rethymnon and Heraklion in the centre and Lasithi in the east. Starting from Rethymnon, thanks to the dense road network, with the main one being the National Road that traverses the island in parallel with its northern coast, you can visit any part of the island in only a short period of time.

ACQUAINTANCE
WITH NATURE

NATURAL GEOGRAPHY-CLIMATE
FLORA
THE OLIVE TREE
FAUNA
CAVES
GORGES
AREAS OF NATURAL BEAUTY
BEACHES

Natural Geography Climate

R ethymno is one of the four prefectures of Crete. It is situated between the prefectures of Chania and Heraklion, abutting the Cretan Sea in the north and the Libyan Sea in the south. Its capital, which has the same name as the prefecture, is situated 58 km from the town of Chania and 78 km from the town of Heraklion. The central part of the town of Rethymno is built on the cape of the northern shore of the prefecture. The developing town stretches along the northern sandy beach, which has a total length of 13 km, whilst a range of low mountains of which the highest peak is Mount Vrysina (858 m), rises up south of the town centre. The prefecture terrain is mainly mountainous with small but interesting morphological changes such as imposing gorges, a large number of caves, lush valleys and small rivers. Areas of flat land can be found primarily in the northern coastal region as well as between massifs. Equally restricted is the number of rivers. The Geropotamos, or Avlopotamos from the mountainous area of Mylopotamos flows into the sea west of Panormo, and the Megalo Potamos flows into the lagoon at Preveli. All the other rivers in the northern part of the prefecture are of minor importance and usually carry water during the winter period only. Thus mountains and mountain ranges dominate the terrestrial morphology of the prefecture. In the east Mount Ida, or Psiloritis, rises up. With a height of 2456 m it is the highest peak of the island of Crete, its massif covering approximately

The winds on the north and south coast allow excellent surfing

There is a view of the sea from almost everywhere

1/5 of the total territory of the prefecture. The mountain range of Kedros (1777 m) rises southwest of Psiloritis. Together the two massifs border the beautiful valley of Amari. On the northeasterly border of the prefecture is Mount Kouloukounas, also called Talaia Mountain (1083 m), and south of the town of Rethymno is Mount Vrysinas (858 m). Mount Kryoneritis (1312 m) lies south west of the town and is the most

MONTH	AIR	SEA
January	13	15
February	13	15
March	14	16
April	17	19
May	20	21
June	24	24
July	26	26
August	26	26
September	24	23
October	20	22
November	17	19
December	14	16

Average sea temperatures and air temperatures

easterly peak in Crete's second large massif, the White Mountains.

Due to the hot summers and the long periods of rainfall, which lasts from autumn almost to April, the climate can be characterised as "temperate Mediterranean". Temperatures range around 14^0 C in winter and 29^0 C in summer.

Furthermore, strong northerly and southerly winds play a significant role in this area with respect to meteorological phenomena.

Mount Psiloritis

Flora

As well as trees and plants, which can also be found in other regions of Greece and the wider Mediterranean area, there are a large number of plants endemic to the island. This can be explained by the geological isolation of the island, which has facilitated the development of local species since ancient times. Out of an estimated number of 2000 species of plants 160 are endemic and grow exclusively on the island. Unfortunately, compared to periods of the past, the vegetation of today has been diminished to a large degree. Mountains which previously had lush vegetation such as Psiloritis and Ida (which was planted with trees) are today almost bare mainly due to uncontrolled pasturing of sheep and goats, and fire. At the same time the few areas of flat land had to be used for agricultural farming, and in some coastal areas green-houses were built with the result

A wild goat chewing dittany in order to heal the wound inflicted by an arrow (O.Dapper). The miraculous qualities of dittany have been known since ancient times

that the flora and fauna has been restricted to a large degree and many rare species of plants today are in danger of extinction. Since the development of the flora depends on the temperature and the

The Cretan palm tree (Phoenix theophrasti), which is endemic to the island of Crete, can be found in marshy areas where rivers flow into the sea, such as at the Lake of Preveli

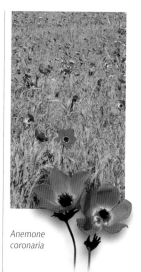

Anemone
coronaria

factors. Thus in the **coastal area** humidity and the salty air of the sea favour plants such as the sea lily (Pancratium maritimum) the tamarisks (Tamarix cretica) and the famous Cretan palm (Phoenix theofrastii). In the **area of flat land**, which goes up to a height of 300 m, the Mediterranean macchie can be found including lentisk (Pistacia lentiscus), holm-oak (Quercus coccifera), oleander (Nerium oleander), Vitex agnus-castus, camomile (Chamomilla recutita), mint (Mentha spicata), myrtle (Myrtus communis), heather (Erica), Daucus carota, wild celery (Smyrnium), hollyhock (Alcea pallida cretica), the common poppy (Papaver rhoeas), Cistus incanus-creticus, as well as Cretan ebony (Ebenus cretica). **The semi-mountainous**

The orchids of Crete, minute and beautiful, imitate the insects in order to attract them

morphology of the terrain, its classification is based on altitude, which influences the above-mentioned

Iris cretensis

area goes up to a height of 800m approximately and includes shrubbery such as the holm-oak (Quercus coccifera), the lentisk (Pistacia lentiscus), thyme (Thymus capitatus), the Arbutus unedo, the Phlomis cretica, the maple-tree (Acer sempervirens), the bryony (Bryonia cretica), the Spartium junceum, the Styrax officinalis, and many others. Wild flowers include Cretan cyclamen (Cyclamen creticum), iris (Iris cretica), Dracungulus, gladiola (Gladiolus italicus), tulips (Tulipa orphanidea), hyacinth (Muscari commosum), various

Pine forest in the area of the Arkadi Monastery

Cistus Creticus, well known as laudanum

species of Cretan orchids as well as locust-trees (Ceratonia siliqua) and oak-trees (Quercus).
The area between 800 and

(Erysimum creticum), tulips (Tulipa cretica), wild Cretan wormwood (Achillia cretica), wild violets (Viola cretica), crocuses (Crocus oreocreticus) and many others.
Of particular interest is the flora of the gorges, which reveals a splendid array of wild

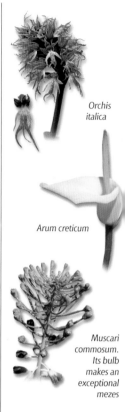

Orchis italica

Arum creticum

The sea-lily (Pancratium maritimum)

The flower and root of the orchid with the characteristic shape of the testes from which the plant took its name. Drawing by J.P. de Tournefort

1800 m of height is known as the **mountainous area**. Here we meet holm-oaks (Quercus coccifera), the Cretan maple-tree (Acer sempervirens) as well as shrubs and wildflowers such as yellow violets

flowers and shrubs, many of which are rare species and endemic to the island. They have been preserved from human intervention, because access to this area is difficult and therefore the environment has maintained its original wildness. Here you can see the entire spectrum of species referred to in the above-mentioned areas, since the gorges start in the mountainous and

Muscari commosum. Its bulb makes an exceptional mezes

semi-mountainous area and end up at sea level. Furthermore, if you are lucky, you might also come across the famous Cretan Diktamo (Origanum dictamus). Finally, in marshy areas, which develop in the coastal zones where rivers empty into the sea as for example at the Lagoon of Preveli, you can find the Cretan palm-tree (Phoenix theophrastii), which is also endemic to Crete.

The plain of Yus in spring. This area teems with orchids, tulips, irises and anemones

Crocus oreocreticus

14

The Olive Tree

Archaeological records as well as historical sources give evidence of the fact that the history of Crete is closely connected with the olive tree and with its basic product of olive oil. Archaeological findings from Knossos have proved that as early as the Minoan period the fruit of the olive tree was processed in order to produce olive oil, which was stored in large earthenware jars and amphorae and often exported to the Aegean islands and to the Greek mainland. However, apart from for the economic profit the tree provided, it was also worshipped as a sacred tree and the olive oil was offered to the gods and to the dead. It was also used for medical and athletic purposes, while in ever day life it was used as the basic component for nourishment, lighting and heating. Thus, from ancient times up until now the olive tree and its blessed fruit have been the symbol of wisdom, of peace, of health and of power. During recent years international medicine and dietetics recommend olive oil as being essential for healthy nutrition and a long life. Due to its Mediterranean climate Crete is predetermined for the

The old olive mill at Arkadi Monastery in Kapsaliana

development of olive trees, which grow in both valleys and mountainous areas and fruit in winter. There are millions of olive trees on the island and thousands of families make a living from cultivating these trees. Both the climate and the composition of the Cretan soil guarantee the fine aroma and superb flavour of the Cretan olive oil, which is internationally acknowledged for its high quality. The prefecture of Rethymno boasts an abundance of olive groves and the production of olive oil is one of the inhabitant's main activities. The sorts of olives that are cultivated are mainly "chondrolies", some "koroneikes" and a

The Cretan olive oil represents the elixir for a long life span

The olive grove in the area of Adele in the Municipality of Arkadi is thought to be one of the largest in the Mediterranean

Ideograms in linear B representing in turn: the olive tree, the oil and the fruit

few "tsounates". These varieties produce olive oil as well as edible olives of excellent quality. The famous olive grove near Adele in the Municipality of Arkadi, which stretches in a vast flat and semi-mountainous area, is considered one of the largest olive groves in the Mediterranean.

The area of Rethymno and generally the entire island of Crete has always been closely linked with the olive tree and the production of olive oil.

Oil-press at Argyroupoli in Rethymno, as captured by the lens of the traveller, Spratt. "Travels and Researches in Crete" by Captain T.A.B. Spratt, London 1865

Fauna

M uch of the same facts can be applied to the fauna as to the flora, since the development of the fauna depends on environmental factors as well as altitude and temperature. Therefore, we shall classify the animals

and the birds, which have their habitat in Crete and more precisely in the prefecture of Rethymno, according to the zones of altitude. In the coastal area and primarily on the rocky shores the famous sea gull nests as well as the falcon (Falco eleonore), which comes from Africa to Crete during the summer months. Furthermore the well-known sea turtle Caretta caretta lays its eggs on the sandy beaches.

In the area of flat land, that is, in the valleys and on low hills, you can find hares, weasels, badgers, hedgehogs, voles (Apodeus sylvaticus-creticus) and bats as well as birds such as sparrows (Passer domesticus), goldfinches (Carduelis carduelis), swallows (Delichon urbica), carrion crows (Corvus corone), linnets (Fringila coelembs) and many others. The same species of animals and birds can also be found in the semi-mountainous area, as well as certain species of predatory birds such as the crow (Corvus corax) and the blackbird (Turbus

merula).

However, the realm of all predatory birds such as the harrier eagle (Gypaetus barbatus) and all the other above-mentioned species is the mountainous area. There, the Cretan wild goat (Capra aegagrus) and the Cretan wild cat (Felix silvestris), which are both in danger of extinction, have their habitat.

The partridge, a characteristic sight in the mountains

The sea-turtle caretta-caretta

Starfish and other species from the marine environment which one can frequently come across on the beaches of Rethymnon

caretta-caretta

Gypaetus barbatus (Museum of Natural History of Crete)

The Cretan wildcat (Felix silvestris). Although it had been believed to be extinct, during recent years it has noticeably reappeared

The green lizard with the characteristic three lines on its saddle, frequently found in the thorn bushes endemic to Crete

Cretan wild goat

The fish species Sparisonea (escarus)cratense. Drawing by J.P. de Tournefort

Caves

The mountains of the Rethymno prefecture are exceptionally rich in caves, there being some 850 in all. Many of these caves are of particular interest archaeologically, historically, folkloric or even just of natural beauty. The most famous caves of the prefecture are those of Gerani, of Simonelli, west of the town of Rethymno, of Aghios Antonios near the village of Patsos in the district of Amari, of Melidoni, as well as the cave of Ideon Andron, of Moungri Sison, of Sfendoni near the village of Zoniana and others.

The Ideon Andron is situated on the Nida plateau of Mount Psiloritis, 24 km from the village of Anoghia and 78 km from the town of Rethymno. Initially its extraordinary large entrance impresses visitors to the Ideon Andron, which is at a height of 1538 m. The cave itself is of particularly large dimensions, with a vast central hall and a gallery of 22 m in length. The cave, in which Zeus was raised according to mythology, represented an important place of worship in both the Minoan and the Roman period. The excavation works that were carried out in the interior of the cave revealed an abundance of important finds such as ceramics, gold jewellery, metal objects and of course the famous bronze shields. Since research is still in progress the cave cannot be visited.

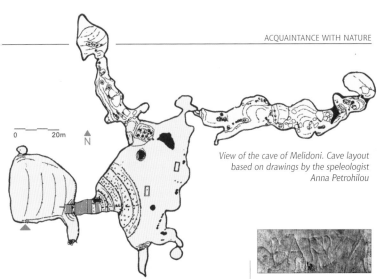

View of the cave of Melidoni. Cave layout based on drawings by the speleologist Anna Petrohilou

Carvings in the Melidoni Cave

inscription gives evidence of the fact that Hermes was worshipped in this cave. It also played an important role during modern times, more precisely during the Turkish occupation. In January 1834, the Turks besieged the cave, where 370 inhabitants of the village of Melidoni had found shelter, set it on fire and suffocated everybody in it. Their bones are preserved in the memorial

Excavation works, which continue to be effected in the cave of **Melidoni**, have proved that the cave was used as a central place of worship from the early Neolithic age up until the Roman period. An

The Melidoni Cave by Pashley

on Andron. The imposing entrance

The cave of Aghios Antonios in Patsos

Stalagmite columns in Moungri Cave

sarcophagus situated in the first hall. The cave is open to visitors.

The **Gerani** cave displays magnificent stalagmites and boasts 6 halls. Apart from three human skeletons archaeological research has brought to light a variety of bone and stone tools dating back to the Neolithic period. Furthermore important material of palaeontological interest was found, probably relics of more than 100 endemic deer, which must have died towards the end of the Pleistocene period. The human skeletons belonged to people who were probably trapped in the cave, perhaps due to an earthquake.

The cave of **S(f)endoni** near the village of Zoniana in the district of Mylopotamos (47 km from Rethymno in the direction of Perama - Axos) displays 14 halls, richly ornamented with stalactites and stalagmites. It is 550 m long and covers a total of 3,330 sq.m. During recent years archaeological research has uncovered installations dating back to the Neolithic period in the interior of the cave.

The cave of **Aghios Antonios** near the village of Patsos also represents a place of dedication as has been proved by archaeological research. It was used as an important centre of worship from the Late Minoan up until the Roman period. An inscription that was found in the cave testifies that Hermes Kraneos was worshipped here. The church in the interior of the cave is dedicated to Aghios Antonios, the patron of the children. The cave is open to visitors.

Sea caves between Panormo and Skaleta

Sfendoni / Sendoni cave richly decorated with stalactites and stalagmites.
The cave has been developed and can be visited by the public.

Gorges

G orges of extraordinary beauty traverse the mountains and mountain

Exit from the Kourtaliotiko Gorge at Preveli

ranges of the prefecture: The ravine of **Kourtaliotis**, which is 3 km long, ends at the famous Lagoon of Preveli; the ravine of **Kotsifou**, which starts at the village of Kannevos and ends near the village of Sellia; the gorge of **Patsos**, in the Amari district; the gorge of **Prasses**, which ends at the village of Platanias at the north coast east of the town of Rethymno; the gorge of **Arkadi** and a number of smaller ones. The Gorge of **Kourtaliotis** with its imposing precipices

The Gorge of Kourtaliotis

reaching to a height of 600 m starts shortly after the village of Koxare and ends at the Lagoon of Preveli. This magnificent gorge is worth visiting. Approximately half way through the gorge and on the left-hand side of the road from Koxare to Asomatos are steps, which lead down to the bottom of the gorge and to the chapel of Aghios Nikolaos. The river Megalos Potamos runs through the gorge, which at this point is called river Kourtaliotis.

The Gorge of Kotsifou

The Gorge of **Kotsifou** begins at the village of Kannevos and ends at the village of Plakias. Just 10 m wide at the entrance, the beginning of this gorge is very narrow, however, eventually the gorge widens out to 600m. It is 1,800m long in total and its almost perpendicular walls reach a height of 600 m. A small chapel built into a rocky cavity is situated in the gorge.

The gorge of **Patsos** is easy

The Church of Aghios Nikolaos in the Kourtaliotis Gorge

The gorge of Moundros ▶

to walk through. Both the gorge and the cave, which hosts the Church of Aghios Antonios, have been improved by the Forest authority and are an excellent destination for short tours and a picnic.

The gorge of **Arkadi** starts at the Arkadi Monastery and leads you through a magnificent landscape to the village of Pikri, which boasts important elements of Venetian architecture. Finally, the **Prassano** Gorge, which starts south of the village of Prasses, offers you a three-hours walk. Its impressive rock faces and a few rather difficult points of access make this tour particularly interesting.

The Gorge of Patso

Arkadi Gorge is a real paradise for nature lovers and one place where, inter alia, you can find interesting fossils

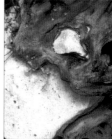

The old bridge at the exit from Prasses Gorge in the area of modern-day Platania

The Gorge of Prasses ▶

Areas of Natural Beauty

R ethymno is characterised by a variety contrasts.

mentioned above, we have selected a few areas of particular natural beauty, which we are certain the visitor will enjoy.

In order to get there you follow the road to the monastery of Preveli. Shortly before the monastery a track on your

The famed sculpture "O Antartis" on the Nida Plateau, a work by Karina Raeck

The Nida plateau

The observatory on the Skinaka peak on Mount Psiloritis

left-hand-side leads down to a parking place. From this point on you will have to walk down to the sandy beach, where a remarkable, almost tropical landscape

Flourishing valleys succeed harsh, mountainous areas, and imposing, rocky shores follow endless sandy beaches. Each area has its own, distinct kind of beauty. Apart from the gorges and caves, which have separately been

Lagoon of Preveli: At the point where the river Megalos Potamos empties into the sea and the gorge of Kourtaliotis ends are the famous Lagoon of Preveli and the beach of Finikas.

On the Nida plateau, which is used in summer as pastureland, you will find the famous 'mitata', the vaulted buildings made from stone, where the shepherds live. The Nida plateau also offers a ski centre, which is open during the winter months

In Argyroupoli the area of Agia Dynami stands out not only for its babbling waters but also for its picnic areas and taverns

The gigantic plane tree at the location known as "Five Virgins" (Pende Parthenes) in Argyroupoli where apart from the magnificent natural landscape one can also visit the Roman antiquities brought to light by archaeological excavations over recent years

with numerous palm-trees makes up for any inconveniences. The river which flows into the sea, combined with the natural vegetation represent a magnificent sight that you should not miss.

The Nida Plateau: 79 km from Rethymno is the well-known Nida Plateau situated on Mount Psiloritis. Not far from there you will find the Ideon Andron, the cave in which Zeus was housed as a child. On the Nida Plateau, which is used for pasturing during the summer months, you will find the famous "mitata", vaulted stone buildings, in which the shepherds live. Furthermore the Nida Plateau provides skiing facilities during the winter months.

Argyroupoli: Following the old national road from Rethymno in the direction of Chania, after 27 km you arrive at Argyroupoli. The village has been built on the remains of the ancient city of Lappas. The large number of springs in the place of Aghia Dynami as well as the cave with the chapel of the same name is worth visiting.

Preveli Beach

Beaches

Rethymno Beach: Organised sandy beach more than 20 km long, stretching from the town of Rethymno in an easterly direction towards the areas of Perivolia, Platanes,

The Prefecture of Rethymno is ideal for summer holidays since it boasts a large number of beautiful and clean beaches. Magnificent sandy beaches can be visited on the north coast, at the Cretan Sea as well as on the south coast of the island, at the Libyan Sea. We would like to detail below some of the more characteristic beaches:

Adelianos Kampos, Skaleta.

Episkopi Beach: Large sandy beach west of Rethymno, partly organised.

Panormo: This coastal village is situated 20 km east of Rethymno. It boasts an organised beach as well as a variety of tavernas, hotels and rooms right by the sea.

Bali: Nestling in the surrounding mountains of the bay of Bali you will find the coastal village of the same name 34 km east of Rethymno. Visitors may choose from which of the small inlets to enjoy bathing at organised beaches. The area offers a large number of tavernas, hotels and rooms.

Plakias: The village of Plakias is situated 40 km south of Rethymno. This resort boasts a superb sandy beach, and the well-organised infrastructure includes hotels, rooms, tavernas and restaurants. The organised beach offers both bathing and various water sports.

Souda Plakias: Organised, sandy beach west of the village of Plakias. A few tavernas are situated close to the beach, where rooms are also available.

Damnoni: Organised sandy beach west of the village of Plakias and south of the town of Rethymno. It offers a few tavernas and rooms

The famed Triopetra beach south of Rethymnon, has taken its name from the three characteristic rocks in the sea

Damnoni, as seen from the beach "Mikro Ammoudi"

are also available.

Ammoudi: Small sandy beach near Damnoni not organised and fairly isolated.

Preveli Lagoon: 38km south of Rethymno, shortly before you arrive at the historic Monastery of Preveli, a track on the left hand side leads downhill to a parking place. After approximately 15-minutes downhill walk you arrive at the beautiful sandy beach with palm trees, where the River Kourtaliotis empties into the sea.

Triopetra: The beach of Triopetra, which was named after the three distinctive rocks in the sea, is situated approximately 50 km south of Rethymno. Follow the road to Aghia

Galini and turn left after 40 km in the direction of Akoumia. Continue until you arrive at the huge sandy beach, which is not organised and fairly isolated.

Aghios Pavlos: The magnificent sandy beach of Aghios Pavlos is found 58km south of Rethymno. Follow the road to Aghia Galini and after 46km turn right at the crossroads of the village of Kria Vrissi. Continue until you arrive at the seaside. Bathing in one of the isolated inlets, which have formed between the rocks, and seeing the sand dunes will be an unforgettable experience. In the village

of the same name you will find rooms and tavernas.

Aghia Galini: This resort is situated 58km south of Rethymno. Apart from the plentiful tourist infrastructure the village also boasts beautiful and clean beaches, which are situated in various picturesque inlets in the area.

Korakas: This beach is also situated on the south coast, more precisely south of the village of Rodakino, 42km from Rethymno. The sandy beach of Korakas is organised and the area offers hotels, as well as a large variety of rooms and tavernas.

"Mikro Ammoudi"
The isolated beaches may not have the facilities of the organised beaches, however they offer quiet and crystal clear water

The extensive beach at Episkopi, west of the city of Rethymnon

Rethymno Beach.
Organised beaches offer umbrellas, sun-beds and water sports. Most of them have been awarded the
Blue Flag and provide lifeguards

Panormo Beach

Plakias

3500 YEARS OF CIVILIZATION

MYTHOLOGY
HISTORY
ARCHAEOLOGICAL SITES
CHURCHES
MONASTERIES
VENETIAN MONUMENTS
MUSEUMS
FESTIVAL

Mythology

The sun and the moon were worshipped in many places on Crete. This was the reason why a large variety of mythical characters were created such as Minos and Pasiphae, Zeus and Europa, Talos, Daedalus, the Minotaur, the Labyrinth, Ariadne and Diktynna or Vritomartes. Furthermore, the domination and power of the Minoan people, who had expanded on the Cycladic islands as well as on the East Mediterranean shores, helped to create myths such as that of Radamanthys,

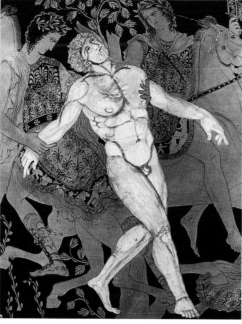

The goat "Amaltheia" on a Roman coin

of Sarpedona, of Deukalion, of Idomenea, of Miletos and of other descendants of Minos. There are two main areas in the prefecture of Rethymno, which are closely connected with Cretan mythology: The Ideon Antron on Psiloritis and the Talaea Mountains, which today are called Mount Kouloukounas and are situated in the north-eastern part of the prefecture.

In the sacred cave on the Ida Mountain, which was predestined to become the most important centre of worship of the ancient world, Zeus, the most powerful of the gods, was born and raised. According to the myth, Kronos, the king of the heavens and father of Zeus, swallowed his children out of fear that one of them might become stronger than him and deprive him of his

The name of the Talaea Mountains refers to the giant Talos, who played an important role in Cretan mythology. Talos was the guardian of the island of Crete. He circumnavigated it three times a day in order to protect it from intruders. This giant, who was made of bronze and had a unique vein running from his neck to his heel, was invention of Hephaestus. Talos was unarmed, however he was able to hurl enormous rocks at hostile vessels when they approached Crete, while at the same time his bronze body glowed so that everything he touched was destroyed by fire. He was also responsible for the laws being obeyed in the country. During his walks through the island he was holding the plaques in his hands, on which the laws were written. This mythical giant would never have died, if it had not been for the Argonauts who passed the island on the vessel "Argo" and Medea, the witch, who helped them escape Talos' destructive blow. She kept him immobile so that she could approach him and take away the small bronze pin at his heel, which sealed the unique vein of his body. Thus the "blood of the gods" ran from his body and the hero collapsed.

Zeus on Mount Ida on an engraving of the Renaissance

The Kourites depicted on a shield from Ideon Andron

power. His wife Rea was inconsolable about her husband's behaviour, since he had already swallowed five of their children. Therefore she decided to fool him in order to save the life of her last child Zeus. Thus, after having given birth, she wrapped up a stone in swaddling clothes and gave it to her husband, who, believing it was a child, swallowed it. Thereupon she hid the child in a cave on Mount Ida, where the legendary Cretan demons, the Kourites danced and struck their bronze shields so that Kronos could not hear the child's crying. While the goat Amalthia nourished the child, a golden dog watched the cave. When Zeus had grown up and was ready to become king, he defeated his father Kronos and forced him to release the other five children from his bowels.

Miniature by the Rethymnon citizen Angelos Vergikios, calligrapher at the court of the French king, Francis I. The map of Crete depicts the Idaian Cave, Rhea with the new-born Zeus, the Kouretes and Cronus. 15th Century AD

37

HISTORY

The existence of human life during the Neolithic period (6000 -2600 BC) is proved by archaeological findings in the Ideon Andron cave on Mount Psiloritis, the Gerani cave west of Rethymnon and the Elenon cave in the Amari district. The greater number of archaeological findings dating back to the **Minoan** period (2600-1100 BC) can be explained by the fact that human existence and activity became more common both in caves as well as in a variety of other dwelling places, the remains of which cover the entire area of the Prefecture and are evidence of every stage of the Minoan period. Dating back to the Early Minoan period (2600-2000 BC) in the Mylopotamos area are the Sentoni Cave in Zoniana and Pyrgi, Eleftherna, in the Municipality of Rethymno are the sites of Chamelevri, and Apodoulou in the Amari district. The palatial installations of Monastiraki in the district of Amari, the settlements of Pera Galinous in the Mylopotamos area, and Stavromenou as well as the caves of Melidoni and Patsos in the Municipality of Rethymno date back to the Middle-Minoan period (2000-1600 BC). Finally, the cemetery of Armeni, the settlement of Zominthos in Anoghia and the place of worship in Fantaxospiliara in the village of Prinos date from the Late Minoan period (1600-1100 BC).

During the **Geometric** and **Daedalian** period (1100-620 BC) important cities such as Eleftherna and Axos (Oaxos), in the Mylopotamos area, flourished, while at the same time a settlement existed on Mount Vrysina, on the plateau of Onythe. Continuous development of the same areas can also be observed during the period of Antiquity (620-500 BC), when works of great artistic value were produced. According to the testimony of more recent sources, during **Classical** (500-330 BC) and **Hellenistic** (330-67 BC) times, the ancient town of Rithimna must have flourished; it was situated in the same place as the modern town of Rethymno is today. Simultaneously, the other large cities of the prefecture, as for example

1. Figurine from the Gerani cave
2. Vessel from Pangalochori
3. Helmet from Axos
4. Roman statue of Dionysos / Satyr
5. Mosaic from Eleftherna
6. Detail from door-frame in Kleidis Street

1 · Late Neolithic period

2800 BC

2 · Minoan period

1100 BC

3 · Geometric Antiquity / Classical / Hellenistic period

67 BC

4 · Roman period

330 BC

5 · Byzantine period

1210 BC

6 · Venetian period. 1669 AC Tourkish occupation

Eleftherna, Axos, Lappa and Syvritos continued to exist during the Hellenistic and the **Graeco-Roman** period (67 BC - 323 AD).

During the **First Byzantine** period (330-824) when the capital of the Roman Empire was transferred to the Byzantium and Constantinople was founded in 330, Crete was included in the East Roman Empire, constituting a separate district, which was governed by a Byzantine general. Henceforth Christianity expanded on the island, and in the 8th century the Cretan Episcopate was integrated with the Patriarchate of Constantinople.

During the early Christian and First Byzantine period a large number of temples were built, archaeologists have discovered many of which. Starting from the year 824 up until 961, the island was governed by the **Arabs**, although very little evidence of this fact was found in the area of Rethymno apart from some Arabian coins, which were found in the village of Giannoudi.

During the **Second Byzantine** period (961-1210) fortification works of the town of Rethymno were started for the first time as we shall see further on. In the year 1211 the long and interesting period of the Venetian occupation began, remains of which can clearly be seen still on all levels in the area of the town of Rethymno.

Marble grave stele with a relief scene of a young hunter. The stele was found in the area of Stavromeno and dates from the 5th century BC. Archaeological Museum of Rethymnon

Ancient Rithymna

Neolithic potsherds, which were found during surface research on the rocky hill of Palaiokastro, reveal the existence of human life during this period. The existence of a settlement here during the Late Minoan period is undoubted. This was proved by the discovery of a chiselled tomb, complete with funeral gifts, in the area of Mastabas, dating back to the last stage of the Late Minoan period (LM III = 1350-1250 BC). However, the most convincing and distinct evidence for the existence of the ancient town of Rethymno, or Rithimna, is given by the inscriptions and coins dating back to the 4th and 3rd century BC; the latter displaying Apollo or Athena on the one side and symbols of the sea such as two dolphins

Coins of Ancient Rithimna

or a trident on the reverse. Furthermore the writers of the 2nd, 3rd and 4th century supply valuable information about Rithimna. Plinios, for example (1st century), and Claudius Ptolemaeus (2nd century) describe the town as being situated between Panormo and Georgioupoli, whilst Claudius Aelianos (3rd century) was the first to mention the existence of the temple of Rokkaia Artemis. The carvings, which were discovered on the natural rock on the Palaiokastro hill, give evidence of the existence of a sanctuary on the hill. Furthermore, there is undoubted evidence that

part of the constructions and buildings the sanctuary consisted of was demolished during the building of the Venetian fortress. The Venetians called the hill "Palaiokastro" (= Old Fortress) which proves that remains of an earlier, fortified building had existed. As to the exact position of ancient Rithimna, nothing can be said with absolute certainty. However, based on a few Venetian written testimonies in combination with archaeological findings in the area of Arkadiou Street and the Customs, it may be concluded that at least during the Hellenistic and Roman period the settlement was situated in the same place as is the town of Rethymno of today. Possibly this also applied to the settlement of the ancient Rithimna, the name of which has been kept alive up until today.

The initial form of Palaiokastro and the opposite land according to K. D. Kalokyris' theory and designs.

Byzantine Period and Venetian Occupation

On the map of Crete from the Isolario by Benedetto Bordone whose first publication took place in 1528 in Venice, the fortified town of Rethymno is marked with the name rettimo. It is obvious that until the early 16th century the fortifications of Rethymnon were intact.

There is little information referring to the town of Rethymno during both the First Byzantine period (325-824) and the period of Arab occupation (824-961). Crete's liberation by Nikiforos Foka in 961, followed by its re-integration into the Byzantine Empire, signaled the beginning of the Second Byzantine Period, which lasted up until the arrival of the Venetians on the island in 1204. At that stage a fortified wall was built around all the buildings, thus constituting the first fortified settlement, the so-called "Castrum Rethemi", which the Venetians later called **Castel Vecchio**. The period of the Venetian occupation formally began in 1204, when Crete was passed over to Bonifatius of Montferrato, who later handed it over to the Venetians. However, in 1206 the Genoese pirate Enrico Pescatore invaded the island, and it was not until as late as 1210 that the Venetians actually succeeded in regaining control of Crete again. The Cretans were in opposition to their conquerors, which resulted in a series of revolutions during the period between 1211 and 1367. Despite the Cretan resistance, the Venetians embarked on successive administrative changes, according to which the island was initially divided into six, and later, during the 14th century, into four sections, with the capitals Chania, Rethymno, Chandakas and Sitia. The Duke (Duca), who had his seat in Chandakas, had sovereign power over the entire island. Rectors (Rettore), who were supported by two Councillors (Consiglieri), were in administrative command of the districts of Chania, Rethymno and Sitia.

This drawing by Z. Magagnatto displays the Castrum Rethemi, which, as is clearly illustrated, was built next to the harbour and east of the hill of Palaiokastro. Neither the fortified wall of Palaiokastro nor the rectangular towers with the two gates have been preserved.

The destruction in the year 1571 and the Cretan Renaissance

After the fall of Constantinople in 1453 the position of the Venetians in the East was gradually weakened. As early as in 1537/38, the architect Michele Sanmicheli from Verona was entrusted with a programme of fortification works, which had already been initiated by the town of Rethymno. His drafts included the land wall of the town, on which the construction works were started in 1540 and completed in 1570.

The attack of the pirate Ulutz-Ali on 7 July in 1571 devastated Rethymno. The Turks found the town deserted, whereupon they plundered it and set it on fire. Most of the houses were burnt; the walls of the Castel Vecchio as well as the land wall, which had only been completed a short time before, had vanished. As a result of these events it was decided to build a fortress on the hill of Palaiokastro, the walls of which should also protect the houses of the town. In 1573, the foundation works of the fortress were realised under the leadership of the Rector Alvise Lando. The architect Sforza Pallavicini drew the initial plans, whilst the supervising mechanical engineer was Gian Paolo Ferrari.

After the fortress had been completed they realised that the space was actually too small to house all the buildings. Consequently it was decided that only the Venetian administration, the Latin Episcopate and the Military authorities should be accommodated within the fortress, while it should merely serve as a place of shelter for the inhabitants in case of emergency.

After several years, when the fortress, the so-called Fortezza, was completed, the Venetians had secured a powerful position on the island. Thus, towards the end of the 16th century the city achieved characteristics of the Renaissance according to Venetian examples. This stage included the construction of luxurious public and private mansions, while at the same time the city achieved a central square (piaz-

Page from the "Great Etymologicon" by Zacharias Kalliergis. Venice, 1499

Page from the "Great Etymologicon" by Zacharias Kalliergis. Venice, 1499

The Venetian character of Rethymno remains almost unaltered, despite the interferences which took place in the last 300 years

*Rethymno and its surroundings.
Depiction on parchment by F. Basilicata, 1618, Venice, Museo Civico Correr.*

za) as did the city of Venice, a club house of the nobility (Loggia), fountains such as the Rimondi fountain, a large sundial, a central street, as well as smaller by-passing roads, which led to the temples, the monasteries, the mansions and the simple houses. Those magnificent buildings were ornamented with a variety of doorframes, some of which were kept simple, whereas others were greatly decorated. They have been preserved up until today

A pirate galley of Barbaria

and give evidence of that brilliant stage in history of the city of Rethymno. During that atmosphere of Renaissance, in which the Hellenic element definitely excelled, the union of two civilisations was accomplished, which influenced the intellectual and artistic domain to a large degree. Scholars such as Markos Mousouros, Zacharias Kalliergis and the brothers Vergikios were highly esteemed in Europe, whilst G. Hortatzis, Troilos and Marinos Tzane Bounialis, the poet of the Cretan War, contributed to the flourishing Cretan literature and were re-

warded for their achievements. On a similar line, Emmanuel Lambardos and Emmanuel Bounialis, both of who were worthy representatives of the so-called Cretan School, also expressed the era of Renaissance in the art of painting.

*Nicholaos Vlastos' logotype.
He was sponsor of
Kalliergis' publications*

M.
FVRGOCHIE
TALO

S.MARIA
SUGA

SCALA DI PASSA·CO·

Drawing by Fr. Basilicata 1618.
Venice, Museo Civico Correr

A cannon from the fortress of Rethymnon

The siege of Rethymno

In 1645 the first Turkish troops landed at Chania and besieged the city immediately. After two months the city surrendered and the great Venetian-Turkish Wars of the 17th century had started. On 29 September 1646 the troops of Hussein Pasha arrived at the fortified walls of the city of Rethymno. These walls had already been weakened because of the many earlier raids led by the Turks, who had previously established themselves in the area of Chania.

Citizens and civilians gathered inside the fortress, where the situation had reached dramatic dimensions due to the plague, the injured, the lack of food and most importantly the lack of ammunition. When the Governor realised that the town could no longer be defended, he raised the white flag and negotiated the capitulation of the city of Rethymno - fortunately on favourable conditions: any of the inhabitants who wished to go to Chandakas were transferred there, while those who wished to stay became subjects of the Sultan. The Fortezza of Rethymnon was surrendered to the Turks on 13 November 1646.

Rethymnon from the East. Marco Boschini (1651)

On this depiction of the town of Rethymno in the 17th century (London, British Museum), appart from the fortress, the buildings, the town and the harbour, we can destinguish the galleys which bombarded the troops that were on the coast.

Venetian galley.
The disagreements among the Venetian officials about the strategy as well as the rough sea led the Venetian fleet to relative inactivity during the Turks' siege.

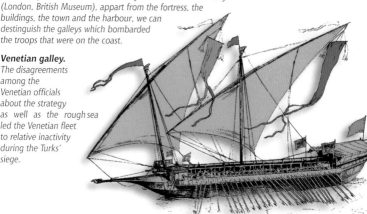

From the Turkish Occupation to Autonomy (1669 - 1897)

The domination of the Turks over the inhabitants of Rethymno (1669-1898) as well as over the rest of Crete, brought many important changes not only in the administrative, economic and population areas, but also in the intellectual and every-day life of the people. By that time the island of Crete was considered large enough to initially be divided into three regions, that of Chandakas, of Rethymno and of Chania, to which that of Lassithi was added later. None of these regions were governed by a Pasha. The image of the town changed radically. The conquerors installed themselves in the Venetian mansions, which they decorated with their own architectural elements. At the same time they started building mosques and minarets, which further emphasised their presence. The so-called "sachnisia", wooden balconies projecting from the façade of the buildings, suddenly appeared in the former Venetian alleys and network of streets, thus giving the city a new character - that of a Moslem town. Many churches were destroyed; others were turned into mosques. As could be expected, these acts led to an intellectual decline. The period of the "Cretan Renaissance" with its flourishing literature and fine arts belonged to the past. Christians were slaughtered and their properties plundered, which resulted in a series of uprisings and revolutions started by the Cretans, among which the most important took place in 1821 in the framework of the general uprising of the Greek people against the Turkish subjugators. However, the Cretans did not succeed in obtaining their freedom in the revolution of 1821. Instead the island was assigned to the Egyptian Vice-Roy Mechmet Ali (1830-1841), a fact, which gave only small relief for the Christian inhabitants of the island, who continued to fight for their

Aïlie-Bech-Baba (Derwich)
Souvenir de Crète (Rethimo)

The so-called "Babas" was a Turkish nobleman who having become a Dervish, returned to Rethymnon and acted as head of the Dervish spiritual centre:

freedom. Over the years their continuous struggles showed a few results with regard to privileges concerning the freedom of religion and the right of holding property. However, the Cretans were not satisfied unless they were completely liberated and united with the Greek mainland. A crucial battle was fought during the Great Cretan Revolution, which lasted for three years, from 1866 to 1869, and

THE CONVENT OF ARKADI, CRETE, LATELY BESIEGED BY THE TURKS AND BLOWN UP BY THE INSURGENTS.

The most important event during their battle for freedom was the dramatic ending of the siege of the Arkadi Monastery. Rather than surrendering to the Turks they decided to lock themselves up in the ammunition storeroom and then blow it up, thus fighting for their freedom in the most heroic way. The man, who set the ammunition room on fire, played a major role in the Arkadi drama. This hero's name was Kostis Yamboudakis from the village of Adele near Rethymno

Celebrations in Rethymnon following liberation in 1898

Cretan soldiers during the period of Autonomy

dominated by the Turks with no change to their situation. Therefore, another revolution followed, that of 1878, and as a result of this one they achieved several religious and political privileges, the most important of them being that a Cretan was allowed to be the General Governor of Crete. However, this did not mean that the situation improved henceforth. On the contrary, from 1890 to 1895 the Turks showed an even more merciless attitude towards the locals, which resulted in the revolution of 1897, and due to this revolution the Cretans finally secured their autonomy

during which the holocaust of the Arkadi Monastery took place. Even after this shattering event and their crucial battle for freedom, the Cretans continued to be

As we can see in Behaeddin's photo (1905), in the early 20th century the Turk-Cretans built a whole town in the area of the fortress.

Vernardou St during the Tourkish period

Autonomy
Union
Modern Times

The commander of Russian forces in Rethymnon, Theodor de Hiostak

The year 1897 was the last year of the Turkish occupation of Crete. In 1898 Russian soldiers took up position on the island and on 9 December Prince Georgios arrived at Chania taking office as High Commissioner. During the same year preparations began to organise Crete as an autonomous state with its own constitution and government. This period of autonomy had positive effects on all levels, mainly however on the economic and intellectual life of Rethymno. A large number of works on infrastructure were carried out, including the construction of luxurious private and public buildings, while at the same time intellectual activities could be observed such as the creation of cinemas and theatres. This creative development continued up until 1 December 1913, when Crete was united with the mainland of Greece. Whilst everything had been proceeding satisfactorily up until then, the union with Greece, which at that time was facing many problems, reversed the creative development of both the town of Rethymno and the entire Island of Crete. Only as late as 1924, after the War of Asia Minor had ended, would the situation improve. The remaining Turkish-Cretan population left the island, while Greek refugees from Asia Minor established themselves on Crete. Their culture and creative spirit was to enrich Rethymno and to provide impetus to a new economic

Post-card, depicting the characteristic atmosphere during the days of Unification

Urban families from Rethymnon society maintained contacts with European centres in order to keep abreast of new trends. Here the "dealings" with the Parisian department store "Au Printemps" are clearly visible

and intellectual prosperity. World War II was probably the most important reason for regression and decline on all levels. The invasion by German parachute commandos and the bombing of the town of Rethymno in May 1941 were only the beginning of a series of battles with a large number of casualties, during which civilians, filled with the euphoria of courage and patriotism, taught the conquerors a lesson. However, the Germans triumphed over Crete and settled down in Rethymno, where they took

The first electricity generating plant in Rethymnon, the so-called "Electriki", was located in what is now Melissinou St

control of the life, the administration and the economy of the town.

The intolerable living conditions as well as the oppression of the conquerors during the period from 1941 to 1944 created a strong resistance movement including Rethymno, with activities in many places of the prefecture. Following

the German occupation a period of poverty and misery began, which lasted up until the decade of the 60's. The installation of electricity also meant a first spark of hope for better days for the people. Since 1960 the town of Rethymno has been following a steady course of development. The expansion of tourism, which started towards the end of the 60's and the first years of the 70's, contributed enormously to this development.

German soldiers "supervise" the town from the Fortezza

ARCHAEOLOGICAL SITES

Archaeological remains were discovered all over the prefecture of Rethymno, dating back from the Stone Age, up until the Roman and Early Christian period. These findings not only imply that this area was geographically important, but also that it had flourished continuously and had arrived at an economic and intellectual peak. Minoan, Geometric and Ancient sites and cemeteries as well as Roman cities and Hellenistic relics have been discovered at many places in the prefecture. The findings in the area of Psiloritis, the sacred Mountain, were particularly concentrated as this place not only hosted but also protected the newborn Zeus from the wrath of his father Kronos. The number of archaeological sites discovered up until today amounts to 350, many of which cannot be visited.

Eleftherna

Excavation at the Orthi Petra cemetery

Excavations in the area of Eleftherna were started, in 1985, when the Department of Archaeology and History of Art of the University of Crete started research on the ancient city and subsequently brought it to light, of which philological texts had already given mention.

As early as 1929, H. Payne, the director of the British Archaeological School, had also carried out minor research in the area. Remains were discovered in the wider area of the two contemporary and neighbouring villages of Eleftherna and Ancient Eleftherna, which are situated in the northern foothills of Psiloritis, at a distance of 24 and 29 kilometres respectively from the town of Rethymno. More specifically, the most important findings have been discovered at three places on a hill, which is situated between two converging streams: at the place of Orthi Petra on the west side of the hill (excavation section III), at the place of Pyrgi on the summit of the hill (excavation section II) and at the place of Katsivelos on the north side of the hill (excavation section I). Further important findings

Supporting walls of the Hellenistic period, Roman buildings and baths, as well as a three - aisled early - Christian basilica with a narthex and a beautiful mosaic displaying geometrical and floral motifs, have been discovered at the excavation site directed by Prof. P. Themelis.

North of the ancient city, following the riverbed, which stretches west of the Pyrgi hill, you will find a bridge dating back to the Hellenistic period. The bridge forms a pointed arch

▌ *The archaeological site of Ancient Eleftherna*

have been discovered in the area of Nisi, near the modern village of "Eleftherna", which mainly include remains of a settlement of the Hellenistic Period. At the place of Orthi Petra, Professor N. Stampolidis, archaeologist and leader of the excavating team, brought to light a necropolis dating back to the Geometric and Ancient Period, as well as Hellenistic and Roman buildings and streets, which had been built on top of earlier constructions. At the place of Pyrgi, on the summit of the hill, where the centre of the ancient city is believed to have been, the archaeologist Professor Ath. Kalpaxis has discovered parts of buildings of the Roman and Early Christian Period. On the east side of the hill, in the area of the modern village of "Ancient Eleftherna", the archaeologist, Professor P. Themelis, discovered a part of the settlement showing all the chronological stages from Pre-historical to Early Christian times. Among others, Hellenistic supporting walls, Roman buildings and baths have been discovered as well as an early Christian basilica with three aisles, boasting a narthex and a superb mosaic displaying geometric and floral motifs.

◄ *Apart from the sites where systematic excavations are carried out in the region of Eleftherna, one can also visit the partly preserved fortified tower, which is situated on the hill and had probably been in use from the Hellenistic up until the Byzantine period*

Late Minoan Cemetery of Armeni

10 km south of the town of Rethymno the famous cemetery of Armeni was discovered, situated near to the village of the same name in a beautiful oak forest, and it dates back to the Late Minoan period (13th / 12th century BC). During the systematic excavation, which was started in 1969, more than 220 tombs were discovered, and excavation has been continued since then with the aim of finding the city belonging to this place. The cemetery consists of burial chambers, which were hewn into the soft natural rock, and which lie from east to west. Long and narrow, hewn corridors lead into the interior of the tombs. Among the tombs discovered up until now only one has been vaulted and built from stone. As well as pottery

Most of the burial chambers had not been looted and still contained a large number of artefacts such as vessels, statuettes, arms, jewellery, tools etc. They were family graves where a relatively large number of dead were left uncovered on the ground or in earthenware shrines

it contained weapons, beads and a periapt displaying an inscription in Linear A script.

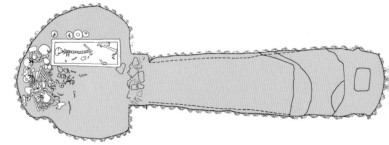

Lappa

During recent years the Supervising Central Committee of Classical and Prehistoric Antiquities has carried out excavations in the modern village of Argyroupoli, where parts of the ancient city of Lappa,

The ruined city. R.Pashley, Travels in Crete, Vol. I

flourished during the Roman period.
In 68 BC Metellus destroyed it. However, after 31 BC, a new, even more magnificent city was built, which boasted not only hot water springs but also its own currency. Recently, a large cemetery dating back to the Roman period has been discovered at the place of "Pente Parthenes". A large number of artefacts discovered during excavations, including two marble statues and a bronze statuette, which were found prior to the systematic search,

Roman statue of Aphrodite from Ancient Lappa. Archaeological Museum of Rethymno

are exhibited in the Archaeological Museum of Rethymno.

considered to date back from the Geometric up until the Roman period, have been discovered in various places. However, most of the findings probably date back to the Hellenistic and early Roman period, a fact that proves that this area had flourished continuously during these particular periods of time. Furthermore, in philological testimonies the city of Lappa is describe as one of the most important cities of West Crete, which

Roman mosaic from the baths in the area brought to light by archaeological excavation

Syvritos

33 km south east of Rethymno the village of Thronos is

Coin from ancient Sivritos, depicting Bacchus on a panther, and Hermes

situated, where at the point of 'Kefala' archaeological research brought to light the remains of the ancient city of Syvritos.

Coins dating back to the period of the ancient city have been discovered during excavation works and are exhibited in the Archaeological Museum of Rethymno.

Axos

O axos, one of the most important cities of ancient Crete, was situated in the area of the modern village of Axos, including the temple of Aphrodite, the prytaneum, tombs and a variety of archaeological relics. The wall of the acropolis, remains of which can still be seen today on the summit of the hill, must have been of particular grandeur. In 1899, the Italian Archaeological School started excavations, which uncovered a variety of findings such as Minoan potsherds, stone vessels, inscriptions and many figurines of a naked female body, which is believed to portray the goddess of Fertility. Furthermore,

and flourished from Late Minoan and Geometric period until Roman and consecutive times. Archaeological pick-axes have brought to light many parts of the ancient city

The cyclopean walls of ancient Oaxos. Pashley, Travels in Crete, 1837

Copper helmet from Axos

remains of buildings dating back to the Classical Period were found, on top of which new constructions had been built, mainly Byzantine churches. The city flourished during both the Roman and the Byzantine Period. During the latter it accommodated the seat of the Episcopate and boasted a large number of churches. At the place of Livada, north east of the village, remains of archaic times have been found, a fact, which indicates the dimensions of ancient Axos.

Another detail implying the importance of Axos is the fact that it had various kinds of currency. Approximately 40 different coins have been recognised, most of which display the head of Apollo or of Zeus, the gods, who were worshipped in ancient Oaxos

Apodoulou

N ear the village of Apodoulou of present day, 54 km from Rethymno and at the place of Tournes, remains of a proto-palatial centre

Vaulted tomb at the entrance to the village of Apodoulou

have been discovered. Sp. Marinatos carried out initial research in 1934. This was followed by research by the German Archaeological Institute during World War II, and since 1985 systematic excavations have been carried out under the supervision of the Greek Ministry of Culture in co-operation with the University of Naples. The archaeological site of Apodoulou must have been of particular importance during ancient times, because it controlled the passage to the Messara plain. Three sets of buildings have been found

Vessel on three legs from Apodoulou

as well as vaulted tombs, one of which includes a corridor 7 m long and three sarcophagi.

View of the archaeological site

Monastiraki

A complex of buildings has been discovered in the village of Monastiraki, which is situated in the valley of Amari, 38 km from Rethymno. It is believed that the settlement was founded in approximately 2000 BC and that it was violently destroyed by either an earthquake or a fire in approximately 1700 BC. This set of buildings includes storehouses, sanctuaries and two archive rooms containing a variety of earthenware stamps, and it is believed to have been a palace. Excavation research was carried out by the German Archaeological Institute during World War II and has been launched again in 1980 by the University of Crete.

Stavromenos

The wider area of the villages of Hamalevri - Pangalochori - Stavromenos and Sfakaki boasts most important archaeological sites. As early as in 1745 the English traveller R. Pococke described the

Minoan sarcophagus. Archaeological Museum of Rethymnon

Casket from a tomb at Pangalochori

area as being identical with the 'Pantomatrion'. In 1918 Efstr. Petroulakis, the curator of the Museum of Rethymno, initiated a first experimental research in the village of Paleokastro. In December of the same year the antiquary Emm. Kaounis discovered a magnificent marble tomb stele dating back to the 5th century B.C. and depicting the relief performance of a young hunter. During the following years, archaeological findings were often haphazardly brought to light in this area.

Goddess with raised hands from Pangalochori

Glass perfume bottles, mainly from graves of the Roman period

Ideon Andron

At a height of 1538 m on the Nida plateau the "Cave of the Shepherd girl"

Gold jewellery from Ideon Andron

is situated. According to the myth Zeus, the father of the gods, was raised and probably even born here. To be more precise, his mother Rea hid the new born child in this cave in order to protect him from his father Kronos, who was in the habit of swallowing his children because he feared

they might deprive him of his power. Hidden in that cave Zeus grew up being fed with the milk of the goat Amalthia, while the "Kourites" covered the child's crying through banging their copper shields. Being closely connected with the myth the cave of Ideon Andron achieved great fame during ancient times and developed into a centre of worship, which lasted over the centuries from the Minoan up until the Late Roman period. Research and excavation works, which the Italian archaeologist Federico Halbherr started

Ideon Andron. The imposing entrance

in 1885, proved that the cave had been used as a sanctuary. From 1983 and henceforth systematic research was continued by the archaeologists Giannis and Efi Sakellarakis.

AUSSICHT von IDA.

CHURCHES

Plethora of churches and monasteries was built in the Prefecture of Rethymno during both the early Christian and the Byzantine period. Byzantine churches amount to an estimated 300 and 30 monasteries. The prevailing architectural style during the early Christian period was that of the "Basilicas", which were distinguished by their wooden roof and their three aisles, of which the middle aisle was raised. Remains of 18 basilicas of that style have been found in Rethymno. However, the architectural style that prevailed during the entire Byzantine period, from the 9th century up until the Venetian occupation, was that of cruciform basilicas with a cupola. Both cruciform, and single-aisled domed churches can be found in various places throughout the prefecture and represent true gems in the countryside of Rethymno. Early Christian and Byzantine churches are not only of great architectural interest, they also display magnificent interior

Agios Ioannis Kentrochori

embellishments: mosaics in early Christian basilicas and frescoes in Byzantine churches. The mosaics usually present geometric forms and motifs taken from the realm of flora and fauna. The frescoes in churches, which were built after the 11th century, depict motifs of narrative character. The techniques used as well as the materials change according to the period of time. This became most obvious during the period of the Cretan Renaissance, more precisely from the 15th century and henceforth, when Byzantine iconography and traditional techniques were

complemented by elements of the Renaissance of western countries. As already mentioned above, the number of churches is so large that at this point we can only introduce a few of the most important examples.

Moni Halevi

Early-Christian basilica of Eleftherna

It is situated within the archaeological site of Ancient Eleftherna, at the point Katsivelos. The basilica, which dates back to the 6th or 7th century has three aisles and is richly ornamented with mosaics.

Early-Christian basilica in Panormo

In 1948 the archaeological axe brought to light the largest early-Christian basilica of Crete south west of the village of Panormo. The basilica of Aghia Sofia had a wooden roof and dates back to the 5th century.

Early-Christian basilica of Goulediana

At the point Onythe, south east of the village of Goulediana this early-Christian basilica with three aisles and beautiful mosaic ornamentation has been discovered. It dates from the 6th or 7th century.

Early-Christian basilica of Thronos

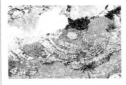

Its remains, mainly mosaics can still be seen today in the Church of the Assumption of the Virgin, which was built on the remains of the early-Christian basilica.

Early-Christian basilica of Vizari

It is situated 2 km from the village of the same name. The basilica with three aisles dates back to the 7th century and was destroyed during an Arab raid in 824.

Aghia Irini (Axos) ▼

An example of the church with a freely shaped cross and a cupola. Imposing blind arches with small pillars in the spandrel of the cupola.

Aghios Ioannis (Episkopi, Province of Mylopotamos)

This integrated cruciform church with a cupola is partly dilapidated and displays frescoes of the Palaeologos technique dating back to the beginning of the 14th century. It was probably the Bishop See of Avlopotamos.

Aghios Georgios (Kalamas)

Integrated cruciform church with a cupola dating back to the middle of the Byzantine period. Presumably it represented the cathedral of the Episcopacy of Kalamon. The frescoes in the narthex show the technique of the Komninoi art of painting and date back to the 12th century.

Aghios Ioannis Theologos (Margarites)

This church dates back to 1383 and displays frescoes painted in the style of Constantinople with characteristics of the Academy technique. Georgios Klados, the founder of the church, is depicted holding a book in his hand.

Sotiras Christos (Ancient Eleftherna)

Cruciform church, where the cross is freely shaped, with a cupola. The wall painting in the cupola, which depicts the Pantocrator, is an example of the art of painting developed during the reign of the Komninoi dynasty. The church dates back to the 12th century.

Aghios Dimitrios (Viran Episkopi)

Church with three aisles, roofed with domes of a basilica, probably see of the Episcopacy of Agriou or Ariou. A fresco depicting St. Dimitrios existed in the tympanum of the entrance.

Aghios Eutychios (Chromonastiri)

Church with a single room and a cupola. It is situated in the area of Perdiki Metochi. The church, of which many frescoes have been preserved, dates back to the 11th century.

Aghios Dimitrios (Aghios Dimitrios)

Church with an integrated cross and a cupola dating back to the 11th century. A plethora of wall paintings has been preserved. It is distinguished by the small sections in the space between the beams of the cross as well as by the pillars, which support the dome.

Kimisi Theotokou (Lambini)

Bei dieser Marienkirche, die sich innerhalb des Dorfes befindet, handelt es sich um eine vollständig erhaltene integrierte Kreuzkirche mit Kuppel. In der Apsis, an ihrer Nordwand, in der Kuppel, am Westbogen an der Süd- und Westwand sind zahlreiche Fresken erhalten, die ins 12. und 14. Jh. datiert werden.

Church of Metamorphosis Sotira (Myrthios, province of Aghios Vassilios)

Situated in the village, with a single room, walls covered with frescoes. Among the frescoes that of the Holy Virgin, holding the infant in the concha of the sanctum, and exactly

below the four Evangelists. Partly preserved depiction of the priest, who founded the church, and his family on the south wall.

Panaghia (Prinos)

This cruciform church with a cupola displays frescoes dating back to the 15th/16th century. An imposing mausoleum is situated in its interior bearing the coat of arms of the Tzagkarolon family.

63

Aghios Georgios (Mourne)

Small, single-room cemetery church with many frescoes from the 14th century.

Kimisi Theotokou (Drymiskos)

The church, which belongs to the old cemetery, can be found west of the village in a small ravine. It is a basilica with a tiled roof and an imposing doorframe. Traces of paint can be observed on its south wall. Remains of frescoes have been preserved in the interior, particularly the Assumption of the Virgin, which is depicted on the arch of the north wall.

Aghios Ioannis Theologos (Kissos)

Church with a single room in the north west part of the village. The interior is covered with frescoes from two periods.

Sotiras Christos (Akoumia)

This small church to which a modern extension was added is situated inside the village. Many frescoes have been preserved, one of them depicting the founder of the church, the priest Michael Koudoumnis. The inscription in the south west corner displays the date of 1389.

Aghia Paraskevi (Melampes)

This well-preserved church with a modern narthex is situated in the village. In its old part some frescoes have been preserved.

Aghios Georgios (Opsigias)

This single-aisled basilica is situated in the village and belongs to the cemetery of Opsigias.
It is distinguished by the doorframe, which shows Venetian elements, while the interior displays remains of frescoes.

Panaghia Kera (Nefs Amari)

Basilica with three aisles and remains of frescoes of the 13th century. Its architecture and sculptural ornaments reveal the influence of Venetian art.

Panaghia (Aghia Paraskevi, province of Amari)

According to the inscription referring to its foundation, the church was built in 1516 as a result of a donation granted by Georgios Varouchas, who is depicted on the west wall together with his wife. The church is ornamented with classical frescoes, which although they display the technique of the capital, they already show the more modern elements of the Cretan School of the 16th century.

Aghios Georgios Xififoros (Bearer of the Sword) (Apodoulou)

The church has a single room with a rectangular ground plan and blind arches at the interior north wall. It is covered with frescoes relating to the ancient technique among which that of Aghios Georgios can be distinguished on a blind arch of the north wall. The church was ornamented by "Anastasios, priest and historian" towards the 14th or 15th century.

Aghia Anna (Nefs Amari)

Apart from frescoes this church with a single aisle displays an inscription revealing the year of foundation as 1225. It is the oldest inscription found in Cretan churches. Although the tradition of Komninos has stayed alive during the first decades of the 13th century, it has achieved a more conservative and provincial level, which is due to the disturbance caused by the Venetian occupation of the island.

Panaghia (Meronas)

The domed basilica has three aisles and belongs to the Kallergis family. It is ornamented with high quality frescoes of the Academic style and the art of the capital. Based on the frescoes and the depiction of the coat of arms of Alexios Kallergis, the church is considered to date back to the period between 1337 and 1341.

Aghia Paraskevi (Assomati) ▶

Cruciform church with a cupola displaying frescoes from the 13th century. At the north wall you will find a tomb above which the remains of three statues in a posture of prayer have been preserved. They represent the benefactors; to the right one of them can clearly be distinguished as Georgios Hortatsis, whereas the figure of his wife has only partly been preserved.

Kimisi Theotokou (Assumption of the Virgin) (Thronos)

Basilica with one aisle built on the ruins of an early-Christian basilica. It boasts frescoes from the 13th and 14th century as well as the of the emblem of the Kallergis family in the lintel.

MONASTERIES

Moni Arkadiou

25 km from the town of Rethymno, at the north-west foot of Psiloritis and at an altitude of approximately 500 m, the Holy Monastery of Arkadi is situated. There are various routes leading to the monastery, each of which is of particular naturalist and historical interest.

According to records the Byzantine Emperor Heraklios founded the Holy Monastery of Arkadi, whereas the Emperor Arkadios, whose name was taken by the monastery, carried out its construction during the 5th century. However, scientists support the opinion that both the monastery's foundation and its name are owed to a monk called

Arkadios. Inscriptions testify that the two-aisled church in the centre of the monastery was built in 1587 and dedicated to Aghios Konstantinos and the Transfiguration of the Saviour. Other inscriptions show that there had existed another church dating back to the 14th century, previous to the church of present day, the restoration of which resulted in the present day church.

The nave is situated in the centre of the square ground plan of the complex, around which the monk cells and outbuildings of the monastery are built. The Monastery of Arkadi became beyond any doubt the symbol of self-sacrifice and freedom during the revolution of 1866-1869, particularly since the besieged inhabitants sacrificed themselves and preferred to die rather than to surrender to the Turks. The brave hand of Kostis Giampoudakis from the village of Adele did not hesitate to set fire to the ammunition chamber, where the besieged had gathered, thus blowing up the entire monastery and turning it into a symbol of bravery and freedom. The sacred banner of the revolution as well as other relics such as monastery utensils, gold embroidered vestments and weapons are on exhibition in the Monastery Museum.

Arkadi Monastery viewed from the east. Copper engraving from 1876

According to the inscription, which has been preserved on the frontal support of the belfry, the church was built in 1587 that is during the period of the Venetian occupation on Crete. This explains the plethora of architectural elements of the Renaissance, which the visitor will notice at first sight. The impressing facade of the church is divided into two sections. The lower section reveals four pairs of columns of Gothic style with Roman elements. Above the Corinthian capitals of the columns a Corinthian entablature can be seen, whilst in between the columns there are three semi-circular arches supported by pilasters. The two corner arches include a circular opening in the centre, the perimeter of which is ornamented with an anthemion. The second section of the facade, that which is extending above the Corinthian entablature, includes a variety of mouldings and ellipsoid openings which are set exactly above the circular openings of the lower section. The belfry towers over the centre of the upper part of the facade, whilst the corners are ornamented with two Gothic pinnacles. The harmonic arrangement of various architectural elements such as Gothic arches and pinnacles, anthemia of the Renaissance, Corinthian mouldings of the late Renaissance and baroque volutes not only makes this façade most impressive, but it also gives evidence of the fact that the architect of the Arkadi Monastery was influenced by the work of architects of the Renaissance, particularly by that of Sebastiano Serlio and Andrea Palladio

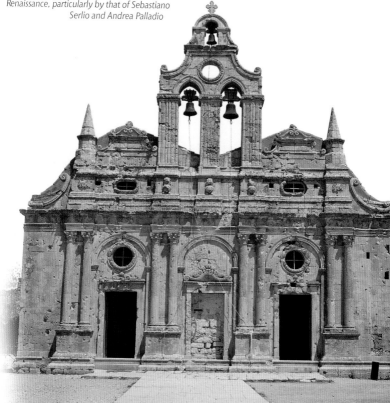

RETHYMNON - THE SOUL OF CRETE

Moni Preveli

The Monastery of Preveli is situated 37 km from Rethymno and includes two monasteries, which are 3 km apart: The "Lower Monastery", which is deserted and the "Back Monastery", which is still run and can be visited. According to tradition the name of the monastery, which has been sanctioned after the 17th century, is either derived from an inhabitant of the village of Preveliana in the prefecture of Heraklio, who, after having committed a murder, found shelter in this area, or it is derived from one of the restorers of the monastery. Towering above the central precinct is the two-aisled church of Aghios Ioannis the Theologist and of the Annunciation. To the West and to the South of the church the cells and the abbot's quarters are situated. The church was built during recent years on the remains of an older Byzantine church. The fountain with the inscription of the foundation year of 1701 is situated on a lower level, as is the Museum of the Monastery, which displays vestments, church utensils, icons etc. During the Turkish occupation the monastery played a significant social and charitable role since it owned various pieces of land, which Christians had donated in order to save them from the grasp of the conquerors. Even a school had been operating inside the monastery, and during the Cretan revolution in 1866 a large number of partisans was given shelter. In 1867 the monastery was completely destroyed by the Turks, and in 1897 it was re-built.

The Monastery of Preveli

Moni Arsaniou

The Monastery of Arsani is situated 12 km east of Rethymno. Apparently a monk called Arsenios founded it during the period of Venetian occupation, and the monastery was named after him. According to another opinion the name is derived from a woman called Arsinoe, who contributed her possessions to the building of the monastery. The cruciform, domed church as it appears today was built in 1888 and is dedicated to Aghios Georgios. The church of present day was built on the remains of an older one, which had been consecrated in 1600. The monastery was restored in 1970, whilst the nave was ornamented with frescoes in approximately 1988/90. The monastery boasts a museum and a congress centre.

68

Moni Atalis Bali

It is situated on a hill and offers a panoramic view on the bay and the coastal village of Bali, which is situated 37 km from Rethymno. It is also called Atali Monastery, a name, which the Venetians had given to the coastal village thus modifying the name of the ancient city of Astalis. Inscriptions testify that the monastery was built during the 17th century, which does not exclude that there had been a monastery there in earlier times. The church is dedicated to Aghios Ioannis. Its façade shows distinct elements of the architecture of the Renaissance. Due to its position and abutting the Bay of Bali, the monastery played an important role

during the revolution of 1821. Later it was deserted, and only as late as 1982 new life was breathed into it when it was restored.

Moni Aghias Irinis

It is situated near the settlement of the same name a few kilometres south of the town of Rethymno in the direction of Roussospiti. This very old monastery is considered to date back to as early as the 14th century. However, at some point it was destroyed and henceforth remained entirely deserted. After restoration works were started in 1989, the monastery was given new life due to the eager activities of the nuns. Today the monastery also represents the heart of folklore traditions, which are protected and preserved by the nuns in the field of handicraft in general and of weaving and embroidering in particular, since it houses a permanent exhibition of needlework produced by the nuns themselves.

Moni Chalevi

It is situated near the village of Chromonastiri 12 km from Rethymno. The large, single-aisled church is dedicated to the Holy Virgin. The year 1864 is carved into the lintel. However, the monastery must have existed as early as the 16th or 17th century. Except for the church

all other buildings are dilapidated and of course the monastery is deserted. Since 1991 it has been annexed to the monastery of Aghia Irini.

Moni Vossakou

Following the old road in the direction of Heraklio, the monastery is situated approximately

50 km from Rethymno, after a north turn to the village of Doxaro. It is dedicated to the Holy Cross. The inscription at the entrance reveals that it was built in 1195, however it was destroyed twice. The present day church is of modern style and was built towards the end of the 19th century. The monastery has a ground plan, which is set out in a parallelogram with buildings arranged around a central yard, in which the church rises up. It was destroyed by the Turks twice, in 1646 and 1821, and was completely

devastated during the decade of 1950. During recent years the monastery showed signs of recovery due to the presence of monks as well as serious attempts to restore and revitalize it.

Moni Diskouriou

Three kilometres before you arrive at the village of Axos in the province of Mylopotamos and after a right turn you will come to Moni Diskouriou, which has been deserted until

recently. Although the old monastery flourished during the period of the Turkish occupation, it repeatedly suffered devastation and was finally deserted. According to the records it had been built on the remains of an ancient

temple or sanctuary of the Dioscuri. In the centre of the yard the Church of Aghios Georgios rises up displaying the icon of the saint, in front of which the stockbreeders settled their disagreements.

Moni Kaloidenas

As its name testifies this monastery is situated in a place with a beautiful view of the valley of Amari. You will arrive there following the road to the village of Ano Meros in the province of Amari. Outside the village follow the turn to Mount Kedros, where the monastery is situated. The Monastery with its church dedicated to the Transfiguration of Christ flourished during the 16th century and during the Turkish occupation. In 1823 it was destroyed by the Turks and henceforth remained deserted. It was recently restored.

Moni Prophet Elias (Roustika)

It is situated south east of the village of Roustika. According to inscriptions construction works were started in 1637. However, since the Turks conquered the city of Rethymno in 1646, the building works were brought to a standstill up until 1667, when they were continued. The monastery played an important role during the entire period of the Turkish occupation, since it was run as a school and took part in the fight for freedom. It was destroyed in 1823 and restored in 1831. After a further destruction in 1866 it was finally restored in its present day shape.

Moni Antifonitrias (Myriokefala)

This monastery is situated in the village of Myriokefala and its nave, which is dedicated to the Holy Virgin, was built in the style of the churches with a freely shaped cross and a dome and dates back to the beginning of the 11th century. Aghios Ioannis the Stranger, who furnished the monastery with icons, utensils and other ecclesiastical objects, which he had brought from Constantinople, founded it. The embellishing frescoes of the 11th century were covered during the 13th century with frescoes of the new Komninian technique, which displayed a much more provincial level. The monastery was run during the entire period of both the Venetian and the Turkish occupation and fell into disuse only as late as the beginning of the 20th century.

Apart from the above-mentioned monasteries in the Prefecture of Rethymno the following monasteries are also worth visiting: The deserted Monastery of Chalepa near the village of Axos, the Monastery of Aghios Antonios in the village of Veni, the Monastery of Peter and Paul in the village of Gallos, which has recently been restored, the Monastery of Sotiras in the neighbourhood of Koumpe in Rethymno, which has been run again since 1935 as well as the Monastery of The Holy Spirit in the area of the village of Kissos.

VENETIAN MONUMENTS

The fortification of the town of Rethymno

When the Venetians came to Rethymno they established themselves in the Castel Vecchio, the first building centre of the town. The Castel Vecchio included a very small area and was surrounded by a fortified wall. Later, the expansion of the settlement beyond that wall demanded the construction of a new wall, which would include a larger area. This was carried out during the period between 1540 and 1570, when the new settlement was fortified according to the drafts of M. Sanmicheli. The new fortification of the building complex included a magnificent entrance gate, the Porta Guora, which led to the central square, where the superb public buildings such as the Loggia, the Rimondi Fountain and the sundial tower were situated. In 1571 Ulutz Ali devastated the wall during one of his raids. Thus it became absolutely vital to fortify the hill of Palaiokastro (Old Castle) and to relocate the entire city there. Many problems had to be solved before the Fortezza was finally built during the period between 1573 and 1578. However, the city was never transferred to the safe area within the walls.

The Great Gate of the city of Rethymno, the Porta Guora, is one of the few remains of the city's initial fortification. The name is derived from the Rettore J. Guoro, who was in office during the period of its construction (1566-1568). It is situated at the entrance of Antistaseos Street and up to the present it has been preserved, 2.60 m wide and with a semi-circular arch. Originally it included a crown in its gable with the relief of the lion of St Marko in the tympanum

The Porta Guora, The Great Gate for the people of Rethymno in the photography by Gerola.

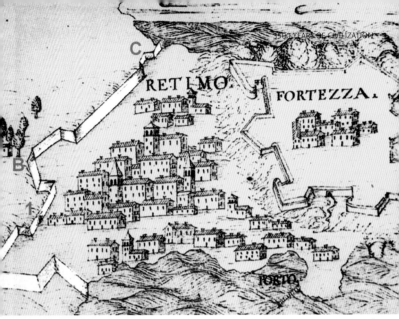

Angelo Oddi's design of 1584 is the only known, which depicts Rethymno after the destruction of 1571. Apart from the fortress which had already been built before the design was made, we can see the fortification surrounding wall of the town with the bastions of Sta Barbara (A), Sta Veneranda (B) and Calergi (C), as well as the Guora Gate (1), which is correctly depicted here (that is in the East of the Sta Veneranda bastion). The part of the wall along the West rocky coast is not depicted. Generally it is not certain at all if the design gives the real picture of the town at that time, as it is known that the town wall after 1571 was abandoned and residences were built on it.

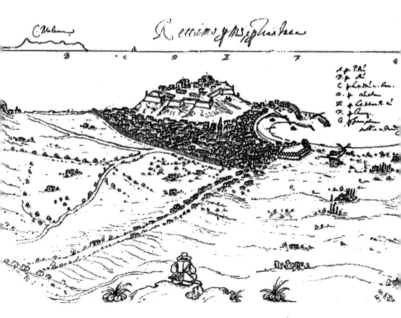

The drawing by an anonymous "painter" in 1629 (Venice, Archivio di Stato) depicts unambiguously the erection of residences on the fortification surrounding wall.

The Fortezza of Rethymno

The Central Gate of the Fortress

Two years after the destruction, on September 1573, the Rector Alvise Lando laid the foundation stone of the castle, which was to be built according to the drafts of Sforza Palavicini. After a large number of modifications, the fortress was finally completed in 1590. The general draft of the fortress provided new forms of defence, which had become necessary, since gunpowder had come into use: The polygonal ground plan included bastions whilst the walls were wider and inclined. In reality however, due to the morphology of the land only three bastions could be built to the South and to the East, while the north wall formed three peaks. In general the draft of the fortification wall was not the best possible, since it limited defensive abilities. The rocky surface, which impeded an appropriate construction, the lack of a moat, the limited free space around the fortress resulting from the inhabitants' refusal to demolish their houses were some of the basic factors, which limited successful defensive action. Contrary to that the infrastructure of the interior space was probably well planned: Public buildings were situated at a distance from the wall, the ammunition storerooms were housed at the safe north side, and a square formed the centre of the fortress. The interior of the fortress accommodated the following basic buildings: the storeroom of the artillery, where canons and weapons were kept, the residence of the Councillors, where one of the city's two Venetian councillors lived, the residence of the Rector, which represented a luxurious, magnificent building in the central square of the fortress. West of the central square and opposite the cathedral the Rector's residential premises were built, part of which have been preserved up to today. The building was founded in 1575 and completed in 1582, and it

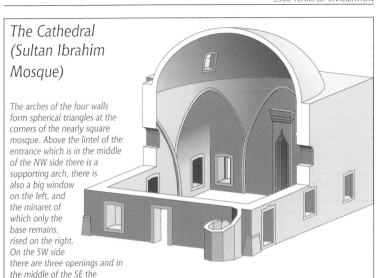

The Cathedral (Sultan Ibrahim Mosque)

The arches of the four walls form spherical triangles at the corners of the nearly square mosque. Above the lintel of the entrance which is in the middle of the NW side there is a supporting arch, there is also a big window on the left, and the minaret of which only the base remains, rised on the right. On the SW side there are three openings and in the middle of the SE the Mihrab niche lies between two windows. On the NE side there are three windows, of which two are lower and the smallest is higher, while on the base of the dome there are four small openings with arched end.

was first occupied by the Rector Anzolo Barocci. He continued to modify the building up until 1584, because he considered it to be too high and exposed on the hill of Aghios Athanassios, in the west of the city. The imposing and luxurious style of the building is testified to in written records of that time referring to 49 doors, 81 windows, two staircases as well as galleries. Unfortunately, none of the buildings of this complex could be preserved, except for part of the prison, which Barocci had built east of the main residence, and for the cathedral, which was situated opposite the remarkable residential complex of buildings and was dedicated to Aghios

The French traveller J. Pitton Tournefort, with this drawing of 1700, gives precious information on the modification brought about by the Turks in the town of Rethymno and on the hill of the fortress: the town is full of minarets, the fortification surrounding wall can not be spotted at all and in the fortress, istead of the Cathedral, a mosque with a minaret were built.

Nikolaos. The temple of Sultan Ibrahim was built on the ruins of the cathedral of San Nicolo during the Turkish occupation. New elements such as the large semi-circular dome, the apse of Michrab in the centre of the southeastern side as well as the minaret, which was built next to the entrance, characterised the transformation of the cathedral into a Muslim temple.

A WALK

The East gate of the fortress with its impressive cannonports and the guardroom at the parapetto consists of a gallery with two arched recesses in the North, which once led to three areas that functioned as guardrooms. After crossing the gallery, on the right we meet the artillery magazine (1) with four arched openings on the ground floor. Opposite it, the wooden staircase leads to the St Paul bastion with the circular guardroom that "observes" almost the whole town of Rethymno and the harbour.

Walking to the West at the point where the second bastion is, we meet the openings of two "wells" that functioned as contramina (2) that is underground galleries for the confrontation of the enemy sapping. In the St Ilias bastion, the "Erofili" theatre every summer, from 1986, "offers hospitality" to the performances and concerts of the "Renaissance Festival" of Rethymnon. The cirular guardroom and the square one, which is unique in the whole fortress, offer panoramic view of the town which extends from sea to sea and our look rests

only on the massif that rises in the South of Rethymnon.

Leaving behind the bastion of St Ilias and walking along the parapetto, we reach the bastion of St Luke with the circular guardroom on its salient. The homonymous cavaliere (3) , which was formed in the centre of the bastion to secure the cover of the fortress against the opposite hills, consists of two buildings in the shape

of Ā, which support the landfills.

Walking to the North, we meet the area of the West auxiliary gate with the cannon emplacement (4) next to it. Following the course of the wall now we are reaching first the Sto Spirito salient with the circular guardroom and then the

one of the two powder-magazines (5) of the fortress. Then in the St Justine salient stands the imposing two-storeyed the Counsillors' residence (6).

In the East, along the North wall, there are the storerooms (7) with the complicated underground areas and the corridor among

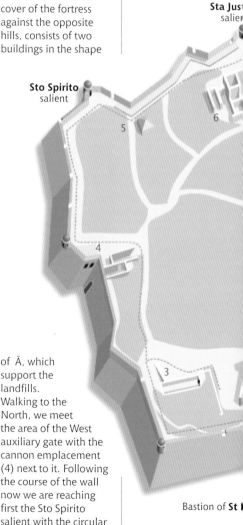

Sto Spirito
salient

Sta Jus
salie

Bastion of **St ▶**

them which leads to the North auxiliary gate. To the South of the storerooms a part of the Rettore's residence (8) is preserved and opposite the Sultan Ibrahim Mosque (9) with the dome, that the Turks built on the site where the Venetians had built their Cathedral. Next to the Mosque is located the probable Bishop's Palace (10) and the conte-mporary little church of Sta Aikaterina (11). Going back to the South wall of the fortress and following its route, we meet the second powder-magazine (12) and the St Salvatore salient with the circular guardroom and the endless view of the sea. Finally, we reach the St Nicholaos bastion with the two guardrooms, the twin building (13), the church of St Theodore of Trichinas (14) (53), the ruins of the private residences (15) and the pit (16) which was constructed after the Venetian period, may be during the Turkish domination or later. The parapetto above the main gate and between the bastions of St Nicholaos and St Paul is impressive. The cannon ports are arched and covered by a semi-circular angle of elevation with its small, decorative end. Walking up the stairs we are again at the main East gate of the Fortezza.

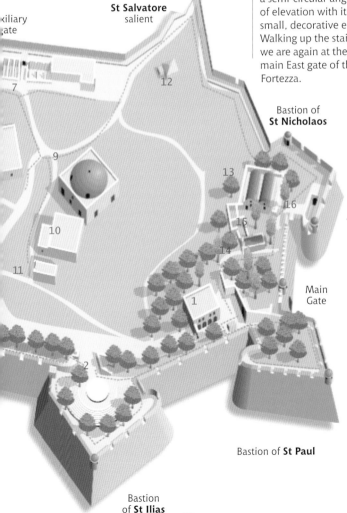

St Salvatore salient

×iliary ;ate

7

12

Bastion of **St Nicholaos**

9

13

16

10

15

14

11

1

Main Gate

2

Bastion of **St Paul**

Bastion of **St Ilias**

77

The fortress of Monopari

recapturing it. One of the fortresses built by Pescatore is the Fortress of Monopari (Bonripario), remnants of which can be seen from the top of the precipitous hill of Kastellos near the village Ano Valsamonero. Being already a natural

After the 4th Crusade Crete was turned over to Bonifatius of Montferrat, who at a later date sold the island to the Venetians. However, in 1206 the Genovese pirate Enrico Pescatore conquered and besieged the island, and only as late as 1210 did the Venetians succeed in

stronghold the site merely demanded the construction of a wall at the north side of the hill, which provided the only access. Although the fort has not been restored, one can clearly distinguish two rows of walls at the north side, including three

towers for the protection of the entrance, as well as the remains of buildings, two of which were probably storerooms, a cistern and a well.

Public Buildings

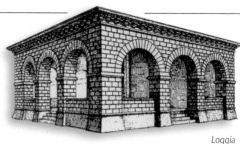

Loggia

The public buildings of Rethymno and also of the entire island of Crete, which had been built during the Venetian occupation, were generally magnificent constructions. On the one hand they served as a successful defence of the area, and on the other hand they gave an air of western architecture, showing at the same time the undisputed predominance of Venice. Apart from fortification works the Venetians provided superb public buildings similar to those, which adorned their hometown, such as loggias, fountains, customs, ports, storehouses etc. During the early years of the Venetian occupation architects and engineers from Venice were especially sent for and entrusted with most of the architectural drafts as well as the supervision of the

construction works. Evetually, some of the Cretans who had taken part in the construction of important buildings were in a position to accomplish work on their own. They were called master builders or "murari" and their work was no different from that of the Venetians.

Remains from the clock tower

The Loggia of Rethymno

The Loggia, situated in the centre of the city, was a magnificent building, where the nobility met to discuss political and economic issues. It dates back to the 16th century and was built according to the plans of the famous Venetian architect Michele Sanmicheli. The well-preserved building has a square ground plan with three vaulted sides

(the west side is not vaulted). It is built of regular sized stones and the projections of the cornice are particularly beautiful. Originally the building was open and had a four-sided roof, qualities which do not apply any more today.

In the Venetian Loggia today one can find and buy authentic copies of antiquities stamped by the Hellenic Ministry of Culture

The Venetian Monastery of St. Barbara converted into a mosque by Kara Mousa Pasha

Aghios Frankiskos

Aghios Frankiskos

This church belonged to a monastery run by Franciscan monks. Apart from the temple two chapels have been preserved which are situated east of the church. The doorframe of the entrance is ornamented with capitals of various orders and deserves particular attention.

The Mosque Neratzes

During Venetian occupation the mosque Neratzes, which today is used as a music school, was the Augustinian church of the Holy Virgin. In 1657 the Turks transformed it into the mosque Gazi Housein or Neratze, and in 1890 they added a large minaret

with two galleries, which was built from the famous stones from the village of Alfa. The chapel of the Holy Virgin, situated at its west side and dedicated to the Body of Christ, was also transformed into a seminary. Outstanding elements of this building are the doorframe and the three domes.

The Rimondi Fountain

A. Rimondi, the Rector of the city, built the famous Rimondi Fountain, which is situated at present day Platanos Square, formerly the centre of Venetian city life, in 1626. The water runs from three spouts in the shape of a lion's head into three sinks. Three small, fluted columns, ornamented with Corinthian capitals are "standing" on the sinks. Above the capitals an entablature can be observed, the middle part of which displays four projections in the shape of the leaves of the acanthus exactly above the columns. Furthermore in this section the words LIBERALITATIS and FONTES are inscribed.

Renaissance street performance at the Rimondi fountain

The Fountain of Roussospiti

The village of Roussospiti, which is situated 10 km from Rethymno, boasts a variety of Venetian buildings such as the famous fountain, which dates back to the 17th century. Gerola described it as "graceful", a characterisation, which, on a closer look, one must agree with. On both sides of the semi-circular concha a pair of small columns are situated, which support the architrave. The spout has the shape of a lion's head.

Detail from the Rimondi Fountain

Private Buildings

N ot only did the Venetian architecture prevail in public buildings but attempts were also made on a similar line in the private building sector. Admittedly, private houses and mansions in the cities and in the countryside could by no means be compared with small Venetian palaces, despite the attempts that were made in that direction, due to economic reasons, but most of all because of the dominant traditional Cretan architecture. Particularly with common private houses the architecture of the Renaissance of western countries was expressed mainly in the façade and more precisely in the doorframe of the entrance. These doorframes, some of which were held simple, others superbly ornamented with pilasters, columns and fine entablatures, represented all architectural orders of the Renaissance: Doric, Ionian, Corinthian and mixed.

The buildings of the city of Rethymno

Private houses in the Venetian quarters of Rethymno, of both simple and luxurious style, still decorate the alleys and streets of the old town up to the present day. As already mentioned, the influence of Renaissance architecture was restricted to the decoration of doorframes, which sometimes showed a rectilinear or semi-circular lintel usually depicting an anthemion in the arch.

The mansion at 154, Arkadiou Street

This lavish mansion was built during the last years of Venetian occupation. An inscription in both Greek and Turkish writing as well as the date 1844 can be observed; the date probably refers to the restoration of the building. The doorframe with its Doric columns and its pediment is of particular beauty.

Doorframe of the residence at 13, Klidis Street

Doorframes often display ornaments in the triangular space beside the semi-circular pediment, as is the case in this building, where the interesting motif of naked children hunting birds is depicted. In the crown of the doorframe with its Corinthian capitals the following inscription can be seen: QUI SPERAT IN DEO SUBLEVABITUR (He who believes in God will be comforted).

Characteristic doors of Rethymnon

Doorframe of the residence at 48, Arkadiou Street

This is one of the most impressive doorframes in the town of Rethymno displaying pilasters with Corinthian capitals and columns with capitals influenced by the Gothic order. Both triangular sides of the semi-circular lintel are ornamented with cupids. The relief of an acanthus in the crown of the arch is also very impressive.

Doorframe of the residence at 30, Vernardou Street

This interesting doorframe displays a Latin inscription dated 1607 as well as the coat of arms of the Clodio family.

The doorframe in the village of Amnatos

Among the many Venetian buildings in the village of Amnatos, which lies 18 km from Rethymno, is a house with a particularly impressive doorframe. The crown of the gable shows the inscription: INITIUM SAPIENTE TIMOR DOMINI (= Beginning of Wisdom Fear of the Lord)

The mansion in the village of Moundros

This Venetian mansion is adorned with a beautiful doorframe, which bears an inscription taken from Virgil's Aeneid. It is said to be a reproduction of the doorframe in the east, central entrance to the Fortezza.

The villa Clodio ▶ in the village of Chromonastiri

This magnificent country residence of the Clodio family is situated 2 km east of the village of Chromonastiri. Recently, restoration has been started on it.

Museums

bastion in front of the central, east gate of the Fortezza. This building represents one of the fortified construction works accomplished by the Turks, who chose this

Goddess with raised hands from Pangalochori

Archaeological Museum of Rethymno

The Archaeological Museum of Rethymno was founded in 1887 by the Society of the Friends of Education. Today it is housed in the pentagonal

location in order to defend the central entrance to the fortress. The archaeological findings are exhibited in the Museum in archaeological order and include the following collections:
1. Late Neolithic and Proto-Minoan findings, mainly vessels, tools and figurines from the Gerani

and Melidoni caves.
2. Objects of the Middle-Minoan period found at the archaeological sites of Monasteraki, Apodoulou and Vryssina. Most interesting in this unit are the collection of seals from Monasteraki and the replica of a settlement from the same area.
3. Findings of the Late Minoan period mainly from the cemetery of Armeni, but also from other areas such as Mastabas, Stavromenos, Pangalochori and Syvritos. The objects include bronze tools and weapons, an impressive serrated helmet, a large variety of ceramics, jewellery and cameos, as well as earthenware figurines, one of

Chest from the post-Minoan cemetery of Armeni. Terracotta chests are impressive for their rich decoration which includes themes inspired by nature as well as religious iconography

Casket from a tomb at Pangalochori

Sculpture of Aphrodite from Argyroupolis. Roman period

metric - Archaic Period mainly from the archaeological sites of Axos and Eleftherna.

5. Objects from the Classical, Hellenistic and Roman Period, mainly from the areas of Stavromenos and Argyroupolis. This unit boasts Roman oil lamps with various depictions, gold jewellery from the area of Stavromenos and glass vessels from the Hellenistic and Roman period.

6. Collection of coins

7. Figurines from Melidoni and Axos as well as pots of unknown origin from the Classical and Hellenistic period.

8. Inscriptions from the area of Eleftherna

9. Collection of sculptures from the areas of Stavromenos, Eleftherna and Argyroupolis.

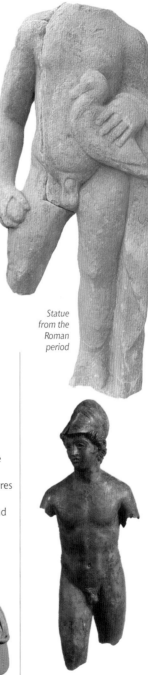

Statue from the Roman period

Helmet from the post-Minoan cemetery of Armeni

which depicts the famous goddess with raised hands from Pangalochori. Furthermore, the earthenware urns with floral and geometrical ornaments, mainly finds from the cemetery of Armeni, are also interesting.

4. Findings of the Geo-

Bronze statuette from the Roman period from a shipwreck in the area of Agia Galini

Municipal Gallery "L.Kanakakis"

Rethymno is initiating dynamic activities in the field of periodic exhibitions of local, national and international interest in co-operation with many supporters both Greek and foreign. All events are carried out within the framework of parallel activities such as lectures, educational programmes, speeches, seminars etc. On a similar line the Centre of Contemporary Art- Municipal Gallery "L. Kanakakis" complements its activities with the edition

T he Municipal Gallery "L. Kanakakis" was founded in 1992. From its beginning it was housed in a Venetian building in the heart of the old, historical town of Rethymno, below the Fortezza and the Archaeological Museum (5, Chimaras Street). It houses a permanent exhibition of the work of Lefteris Kanakakis (oil paintings, sketches and aquarelles), thus representing all the stages of his achievements, as well as works of contemporary Greek artists, which cover a broad spectrum of modern Greek art as it has been accomplished from 1950 until today.

In 1995, the town of Rethymno was incorporated into the National Cultural Network and, as a result, the Centre of Contemporary Art was established, which then proceeded to influence the course of activities of the Gallery with respect to modern art. The Centre of Contemporary Art of

Works of Lefteris Kanakakis from the collection of the Gallery

of catalogues and other educational or instructive material. Furthermore, since 1995 art workshops have been operating under the direction of the Centre of Contemporary Art.

VISITING HOURS:
1 April - 31 October:
Tuesday - Friday 09:00 -13:00 & 19:00 - 22:00, Saturday and Sunday 11:00 - 15:00, Monday closed.

1 November - 31 March:
Tuesday - Friday 09:00 - 14:00, Wednesday & Friday 09:00 - 14:00 & 18:00 - 21:00, Saturday - Sunday 10:00 - 15:00, Monday closed.

Historical and Folklore Museum

The Historical and Folklore Museum of Rethymno was founded in 1973 with the aim of collecting and starting research on folklore material from the area of Rethymno. Since 1995 it has been housed in a listed urban Venetian building dating back to the 17th century and situated at 28-30 Vernardou Street. The two-storey building with its interior yard presents a variety of particularly interesting architectural details. The collections in the Museum come from donations and purchases and include among others hand-woven textiles, tools for the art of weaving, embroideries, lacework, ceramics, baskets, items of metalwork, coins, costumes and historical relics. One of the rooms is dedicated to traditional farming and the traditional way of preparing bread in Rethymno, while in another room traditional professions are referred to. The artefacts are exhibited in units and are equipped with explanatory labels in both Greek and English,

Detail of a woollen bedcover.

photographs and drafts according to the demands of a modern museum management.

**Historical and Folklore
Museum in Rethymno
Manouil Vernadou 28-30**

Other museums in Rethymno

Museum of Sea-life

It is housed in the old abbey, which is situated in the old town and has been restored recently. The exhibition represents one of the most important collections in Rethymno including molluscs, sponges, fish and various fossils.

Church Museum

It was founded in 1994 and is situated in Mitropoleos Square. The museum includes ecclesiastical relics dating back from 1816 up until the present, such as church utensils, icons, bells as well as the clock of the belfry, which had been functioning from 1894 up until 1986.

Show-window of the Museum of Sea-Life

FESTIVAL

The Renaissance Festival

Almost all performances are carried out in the "Erofili" Theatre on the Fortress. To walk on the path, which is paved with cobblestone, uphill to the "Fortezza" on a summer evening and to live the delightful moments of a theatre, dancing or music performance is a blissful experience

S ince 1987 the famous Renaissance Festival has been organised by the Municipality of Rethymno each summer. Due to the fact that both the architecture and literature of the Renaissance have worked as a pedestal for the development of the town of Rethymno, it seemed only natural that the town should become the main sponsor of a variety of manifestations aiming at the promotion of both the Cretan and European Renaissance. Over the course of the years all the works of Cretan playwrights have

been performed as well as a large variety of plays by Shakespeare, Moliere, Goldoni and others. Furthermore musicians from all over the world came to Rethymno to perform a wide

Music performance in the Sultan Ibrahim Mosque

range of music, starting from the period of the Renaissance to modern times. On a similar note street performances of the "Comedia del arte" could be seen in the narrow streets and alleys of the old town. Dancing performances, exhibitions of paintings, speeches and cinema complete the framework of the festival activities.

The Erofili Theatre

The Treasure Hunt

The most popular organisation in respect of participation is the Treasure Hunt of Rethymno. It is the favourite game of the locals of all ages and takes place two weeks before Carnival. During this marathon game, which lasts for one day, your brain, your body and your nerves are tested.
The grade of difficulty has reached an unbelievable level, which makes it almost impossible for somebody who is not initiated to take part. However, it is a great experience to watch a group in action.

The Treasure Hunt helped the young people of Rethymno to achieve a profound knowledge of the town's history, to come close to its monuments and to trace every single detail of historical periods. It is worth mentioning that the way the players accomplish a task in this game has become an invariable component.

A similarly important event is the "Children's Treasure Hunt", which takes place a week earlier.
Finally, the Association of Hotel owners in co-operation with the Municipality of Rethymno organises a treasure hunt each summer in the framework of the "International Day of Tourism". Visitors to the town are invited to participate and the winners are awarded 'all included' holidays in Rethymno.

Well-known Greek cartoonists at work for the game. On the right the poster of the year 1999, drawn by Arkas. Poster design of the year 2000 by Dimitris Chantzopoulos (on the left), and of 2001 by Stathis (in the centre)

Carnival in Rethymno

including live music for everyone's taste, as well as titbits and wine. All the locals look forward to the event, since during the last years it has developed into the largest open-air party the town has even known. On the Sunday before the great parade a party is organised for the participating groups, who not only appear dressed up with costumes but they

The first elements of humorous performances in Rethymno during the period of Carnival date back to the beginning of the last century, to the year 1915. Although the social and economic problems of that period did not allow for an established festival as yet, in 1926 and 1933 the first Carnival parades with impressive carriages were organised and incited the inhabitants of Rethymno to rejoice. 1959. The "Travelling Club" of Rethymno reorganised this magnificent tradition, with the result that the Carnival of Rethymno became an established event and is well received on the entire island. People dressed up, playing the guitar and the mandolin arouse an atmosphere of joy and happiness while clouds of confetti are thrown down onto them from the balconies. The people of Rethymno duly pay their respects to "His Majesty the King of Carnival presented in an escapade of unrestrained laughter."

The town of Rethymno organises the grandest carnival on the island of Crete and one of the most impressive of Greece. It is worth mentioning that apart from the magnificent parade various other events take place in the framework of the carnival festivities. On Shrove Thursday a street party is organised on Platano Square and at the Church of Mikri Panaghia

also perform sketches, which the members of each group have written and which refer to the subject they have chosen for the parade. Of course the party, which includes plenty of food, wine and dancing, continues up until the early hours of the morning. On Shrove Friday, two days before the actual Carnival parade is held, one gets a first impression of what it will be like, when the parade passes through the

town at night.
More than 4,000
people have worked
feverishly for
months in order to
present their masks
and carriages on
the great Carnival
parade.
On Shrove Monday
the revival of
traditions and
customs in
picturesque
villages of the
Prefecture of
Rethymno challenges
and invites everybody

to experience an
unforgettable Shrove
Monday.
The villages of Meronas
at the foothills of Mount
Psiloritis and of Melidoni
welcome hundreds of
aficionados of the old
customs, which up
until today include
Carnival games,
happenings and
satires and keep the
memories of earlier
times alive.
Customs such as the
"kidnapping of the
bride", the "Kantis",

the smudging of people,
performed in combination
with good wine and the
music of the lyre are a
successful formula for a
unique experience.

The Cretan Wine Festival

In the coolness of the
Municipal Garden,
the "Travelling Club"
of Rethymno organises
the Cretan Wine Festival
each summer. A rich
programme including

traditional Cretan and
Greek folklore music
groups is offered, thus
illustrating the Greek
way of entertainment
every evening to the
large number of local and
foreign visitors. Wine is
abundantly consumed
since it is free. The visitor
will find choices of wine
from the largest
wine producing companies
of Crete, and he is given
the opportunity to try
almost all the flavours and

varieties of the famous
Cretan wines.

FEASTS AND TRADITIONS

RELIGIOUS HOLIDAYS
AGRICULTURAL HOLIDAYS
THE CRETAN COSTUME
MUSIC AND DANCES
HANDICRAFT
DYEING THE FABRIC
DIET

TRADITION

Religious Holidays

Since ancient times the inhabitants of Rethymno have been renowned for their skills in literature and art, and also for their devotion to traditional work concerning nature, agriculture and stockbreeding. Within this framework they have developed a specific relationship with the tradition, the customs and the way of living of their home country; they carefully keep these things alive in every corner of the prefecture and see to it that they are passed on to their children and grandchildren. Thus both every-day-life and the days such as religious holidays

or holidays arising from the social need for relaxation and entertainment are organised in an environment of continued unchanging values. Traditions relating to celebrations for the worshipping of God, nature, production and life itself represent a very important chapter in the life of the people of Rethymno as well as of all Cretans.

Religious holidays include **Christmas**, Epiphany, carnival festivities, Easter, the Assumption of the Virgin as well as the name days of all saints and are celebrated with particular energy. Christmas is considered a family festivity, which is celebrated in a warm, quiet atmosphere. Fragrances and flavours of traditional cooking and pastry making, special dishes, which decorate the Christmas table are just as much part of it. **Epiphany** is celebrated on 6 January in the ports, where the priests bless the sea by throwing the Holy Cross into the water.

Divers jump into the cold sea, competing with each other in order to catch the cross, while the sirens of large and small boats fill the air joyously. Carnival and Shrove Monday are celebrated in January or February, depending on the date of the Easter celebrations, and mark the beginning of Sarakosti, that is the Lenten period, which lasts for 40 days.

Carnival Sunday (Apokria) is the last day on which meat may be consumed before Lent begins on **Shrove Monday**. On that day people celebrate the event in the country with Lenten food and kite flying. Undoubtedly **Easter** is the most important festival of the Orthodox Church. During this period the religious belief of the people is felt strongly, since Easter celebrations are not restricted to Easter Sunday only, but they also include the previous week, Holy Week, during which

Epiphany in the Venetian port of Rethymno.

The Good Friday funeral bier procession

the ceremonies preparing for the great celebration are carried out. The parish congregates to attend afternoon and evening services. On Good Friday the Epitaph is decorated with fresh, sweet-smelling flowers, and in the evening it is carried through the neighbourhoods followed by the congregation, who chant and scatter roseleaves onto it. The following night, on Easter Saturday, Resurrection is celebrated. The faithful, all equipped with candles, take home the "Holy Light", which has been passed on to the congregation. At home they sit around the festive table in order to enjoy the Mayiritsa and to smash the red painted eggs.

On Easter Sunday people have barbecues in the countryside, grilling lambs and celebrating the Resurrection of Christ as well as the beginning of spring. 15 August, the **Assumption of the Virgin**, is also one of the major holidays of the Orthodox Church, which is combined with the summer holidays and jaunts to the beaches. Religious holidays also include the name days of saints, particularly of those who are the patron saints of towns and villages. The name day of the patron saint of a village is traditionally celebrated with Cretan dances in the village square. These festivities, which usually take place during the summer months, offer the opportunity for holidaymakers and locals to come together and represent a genuine occasion of entertainment for the people living in the country. The Cretan wedding and baptism also belong to the festivities which are closely connected with the Orthodox faith, while at the same time they offer people the opportunity to enjoy themselves and to tighten the bonds between friends and relatives. The **Cretan wedding** is of particular importance since the joyous event is celebrated in high spirits, and sometimes the feast lasts for days. The ceremony starts with the so-called "carrying-away", when the groom, his relatives and his friends set off for the bride's house in order to take her away. This procession is accompanied by a lyre-player and they sing "mantinades", Cretan rhymes, altogether. At the bride's house they meet with the bride's friends and relatives and after the two parties have exchanged "mantinades", the bride is finally given away while pistols are fired into the air. After the church ceremony a wonderful party is organised with Cretan dances, songs and meat and wine in abundance.

A Cretan wedding

Agricultural Holidays

Apart from the religious holidays, the farmers' and stockbreeders' festivities are of similar importance. Such festivities are related to the harvest of agricultural produce, the testing of the produce or stockbreeding procedures. Since the necessary and often hard work could only be accomplished if all the villagers joined together and helped each other, many of these events developed into celebrations. The host organises a feast with music and dancing in order to thank all those who helped accomplish the task. It was the necessity of agricultural tasks that helped the villagers to enhance their life, to develop long-lasting bonds of friendship, to have

During the distilling procedure friends and relatives gather around the cauldron where plentiful food and wine is served and the newly produced raki is tested

Tsikoudia cauldron

fun and to express their enthusiasm and devotion for nature and productivity. In a similar vein the **grape harvest**, which takes place in September, developed into a true festival with a lot of fun and singing, which is continued when the grapes are pressed to

produce wine and raki. The event of **tsikoudia distilling** is also celebrated as the so-called festival of the "kazani" (cauldron). Furthermore the cultivation and harvest of various other produce always offers the opportunity to celebrate as for example during

"Antikristo": a traditional method for roasting food at a baptism in Gerakari

the cherry and walnut harvest and in earlier times during the olive harvest. Another impressive festivity takes place in the area of stockbreeding, when the sheep are sheared in springtime. The stockbreeders of the mountain villages invite their friends and relatives and after the shearing they all celebrate the event with plentiful food and wine, and music and dancing.

Threshing wheat

The shearing

The Cretan costume

U p to today the famous Cretan costume is still worn in several villages as men's everyday wear, as well as being worn as formal wear by men and women on the occasion of traditional celebrations. The multifarious designs display a combination of the arts of weaving and embroidering.

A specialised tailor sews the men's costume, which first appeared during the 16th century and includes the so-called "sariki", a crocheted black scarf, which is wrapped around the head, as well as the "stivania", the boots belonging to the costume. The formal costume was richly embroidered in dark blue or black colours and always included the silver knife and the scarf. Women's traditional costume was introduced during the last 25 years of the 16th century. It appeared in two variations, the "Sfakiani", that is the costume worn in the area of Sfakia, which later became the official costume of the entire island, and the "Anoghiani", which was designed later, approximately in the middle of the 17th century and was mainly worn in the area of Anoghia, in the province of Mylopotamos.

The costumes from Sfakia and Anoghia

Music and Dances

T he Cretan's close relationship to music and dancing can be traced back to the beginning of the history and the myths of the island. In one of the most famous myths, that of the "Kourites" for example it is described that the Kourites, the guardians of the infant Zeus, danced while they beat their shields in order to cover up the infant's crying. Furthermore historical testimonies give evidence of this relationship as well as pieces of art such as the well-known sarcophagus from Aghia Triada, on which for the first time a lyre with seven cords is depicted. With respect to the same issue Homer mentioned the shield of Achilles,

The statue of Kostas Moudakis in a central square of Rethymno

Rodinos and Baxevanis, the legendary duo

which was ornamented with pictures displaying revelry at Knossos. All these testimonies give an exact description of the geographical area where music and dancing were of major importance in every event of people's life, as for example in the event of religious ceremonies, entertainment, birth, marriage, death and even war. The basic instrument of Cretan music, the Cretan lyre, first made its appearance in the 17th century, while the art of playing the lyre became common practice from the 18th century. Of course the initial shape of the instrument was rather

different from that of the lyre of modern times, which the Rethymno citizen Manolis Stagakis built in 1940. The lyre, which is in the shape of a pear as it has always been, was first accompanied by the "boulgari" and only later by the "laouto", the lute, which is still used today. Both the sound and shape of the Cretan lyre and the traditional songs were improved after World War II; undoubtedly the lyre players of Rethymno played an important role in this development. During that period Kostas Mountakis and Thanassis Skordalos, both citizens of Rethymno, were the lyre players to blaze the trail for a worldwide recognition of the traditional Cretan music in the following decades. On a similar line other competent artists of that time as well as of previous years such as Manolis Lagos, Andreas Rodinos and Stelios Foustalieris, the latter performing mainly on the "boulgari", helped to establish Cretan traditional music. Thus to the music of the lyre, the laouto and occasionally of the violin and the guitar the musicians sing "mantinades", which are mainly amorous compositions arranged in couplets. Apart from the mantinades, the "rizitika", which are slow songs of narrative character, are also a widespread variety of Cretan music. Their main subjects are marriage, death, historical events, heroic characters etc. Closely connected to the traditional music and songs as they developed in

the course of time was the art of dancing, which the Cretans and particularly the people from Rethymno, who were distinguished by their gallantry, improved to a large degree. The roots of Cretan dances date back to Minoan times. Contrary to the "syrtos", which is danced in a large circle, the "sousta" is danced by couples. It is an erotic and vigorous dance, which is danced almost on the tip of the toes. Traditional dances, during which men and women wear the superb

Stelios Foustalieris, famed player of the musical instrument "Bulgari"

Cretan costumes, include slow and swift rhythms, however both varieties always show dynamic and imposing postures. Their direct relationship to dances of war becomes evident particularly if they are danced in a circle by a group of men. Following the rhythm of the lyre the dancers gradually improve their technique while they perform the difficult steps of the basic dances such as the 'Pentozalis, the 'Syrtos' and the 'Pidichtos'. The dancer who leads the circle, usually a man, is supported by the right hand of the second dancer and is thus able to perform excellent leaps, the so-called "tsalimia".

Handicraft

Margarites:
At the potter's wheel

R emains of the Minoan civilisation, or at least those artefacts, which the archaeological pickaxe has been able to bring to light and which could be preserved, give the most important evidence of the dextrously produced pieces of handicraft, which the Cretans have accomplished and improved since prehistoric times. Traditional techniques and the feeling for aesthetic creation, which have been developed by their ancestors, are flourishing mainly in the villages up to the present day, resulting in pieces of folklore art of amazing quality. In Rethymno a wide variety of handicrafts such as pottery, basket weaving, woodcarving, stone masonry and of course weaving have been kept alive. Sometimes entire villages are occupied with a particular handicraft, which helps to support their income. Thus, in the village of Margarites (province of Mylopotamos) most of the inhabitants are mainly

Carving "Cretan" furniture

occupied with the art of pottery. They produce both objects for decoration and everyday use. On a similar line in the village of Alfa the art of traditional stone masonry is still flourishing, due to the beautiful

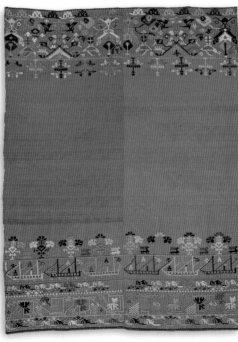

"Patania" - Traditional Cretan woollen blankets: a representative sample of Cretan handicrafts

Hand-woven fabrics at Anoghia

white and relatively soft stone, which is quarried in the area. Since ancient times it has been used as building material, as it offers structural and decorative solutions in architecture. The traditional art of weaving, embroidering and crocheting is still flourishing in the mountain villages of the province of Mylopotamos, in the villages of Anoghia, Zoniana and Livadia as well as in the entire prefecture. Women mainly accomplish these arts in their spare time. The techniques are passed on from mother to daughter, while the dowry is prepared, that is the girl's entire outfit of clothing and linen, which she takes away with her on the day of her wedding. The traditional materials used for weaving include wool, cotton, flax and silk, which the women themselves process, transform into yarn and then use on the loom. Up to today they often use natural colours from plants and wild flowers to dye the yarn.

Rethymnon stitch. The continuation of a tradition

Multi-colored silk embroidery for the woman's costume

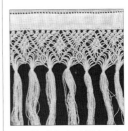

"Desia". the skillful result

Dyeing the Fabric

The earliest information for the process of dyeing textiles with natural dyes is found in literature. Particularly helpful is Pliny (AD 23-79) who describes in detail the process of dyeing with plant extracts. Also Egyptian papyruses of the 3rd and 4th centuries AD mention the three stages of dyeing wool which does not differ greatly from that practiced today in the traditional dyeing of fabrics.

These stages comprise: cleaning the material, immersion in styptic solution (to dry it out) followed by the main dyeing. The colors are either from plants or animals. The main dyeing agents are: Porphyry (purple), which is obtained from sea shells and gives a red iodine color. The use of porphyry in dyeing is known from minoan times. Red which is obtained from the Holly-oak (bug), a type of insect that lives on the leaves of the flax, oak and cedar, the seaweed which is found in abundance on the sea shore and the roots of the Dyer's Madder (rubia tinctoria).

The leaves of the planc tree and the walnut, as well as the green shell of the walnut itself, gives a dark brown colour. The samphire (inula viscosa) which grows as a bush in uncultivated areas, and the fresh leaves of the almond and pomegranate give green. There are many plants which give a yellow dye: Crocus (crocus sativa), the yellow corn marigold (chrysanthemum segetum) which flowers in the fields in autumn, the bark of the pomegranate, the leaves of the chaste tree (vitex agnus castus), the narcissus (narcissus tazetta), cape sorrel (oxalis pes-capare) which flowers from February to April, and the chamomile.

Apart from plant and

1. CROCUS SATIVA
2. RUBIA TINCTORIA
3. SCHILDLAUS
4. INULA VISCOSA
5. CHRYSANTHEMUM SEGETUM
6. KAMILLE
7. VITEX AGNUS CASTUS
8. NARCISSUS TAZETTA
9. OXALIS PES-CAPARE
10. MANDELBAUM
11. PLATANE
12. GRANATAPFELBAUM

animal materials used for dyeing other substances like soot, for black and the rust from iron for brown were used. Indigo was also prepared for blue.

Diet

is no reason to change them. This has been the case regarding Cretan gastronomy, which, despite the long-term presence of various conquerors on the island, has remained unaffected and original. At first sight one could say that Cretan cuisine is simple, including only a few specific dishes. This is true since the secret of Cretan cooking lies in the simplicity of preparation and of the use of only few ingredients, which are plain, precise, clear and, most important, genuine and natural. This applies to the entire island with only very few variations in each area. Naturally the Cretans developed their diet based on the produce, which could be supplied in the area they lived in. Such produce guaranteed the locals both the basic and complete nutrition, which today is recognised as being essential for the proper development of the body as well as for a long life span. Principally, all over Crete people eat various species of wild vegetable, which grow in mountainous areas, either as salad or simply boiled, topping it with local olive oil and natural lemon juice. However, people not only collect wild vegetable, but also the famous snails, which are either cooked with tomato sauce or fried, "boumbourista", that is with rosemary and quenched with wine. Most products needed for proper nutrition come from stockbreeding, which has flourished in the mountainous areas of Crete since ancient times. Sheep and goats supply

Olives and olive oil, the secret for a long life

If customs have endured the passage of time and remained unchanged despite the development of alternatives, then these have met all the needs and there

Graviera (Gruyere), Kefalotyri, Myzithra and Feta

104

both the famous meat, which is also the basic dish of the Cretan menu, and dairy products, of which the island boasts a large variety including excellent milk, various cheeses such as Myzithra, Graviera and Feta as well as the unique 'stakoboutyro' (butter from sheep and/or goat's milk) which is used for pilaff. Apart from sheep and goats each family living in a village also breeds domestic animals such as chickens and rabbits, which provide them with eggs and meat on an everyday basis. Undoubtedly, the local olive oil adds to the special flavour of all Cretan dishes. Together with stockbreeding the production of olive oil represents one of the island's main sources of income. Olive oil is used for cooking and as a dressing for salads, fresh vegetables and pulses, which in combination with the local barley rusk and a few olives often make a complete dish for the Cretan. The famous Cretan 'dakos' is simply this - a delicious and nourishing combination of fresh local products including barley rusks, grated tomatoes, feta cheese, oil and salt. As a dessert the Cretans once again prefer home-made sweets consisting of ingredients of their own production: cheese pies made from Myzithra and brown fried pastry with honey.

Muscari Commosum Bulbs, the co-called "Skordoulaki"

The Cretan "Dakos"

105

ITINERARIES

TOURS IN TOWN
EXPLORING THE PREFECTURE
FOOT & BIKE ROUTES
ON THE E4 PATH

Tours in Town

1.Our tour starts at the **Porta Guora**, also called the Great Gate, at the entrance to Antistaseos Street. The gate represents the only remaining part of the ancient fortified wall of the town of Rethymno. Continuing down Antistaseos St., which is also known as Mikri Agora (Small Market), you will find the church of **Aghios Frangiskos** on your left-hand-side, and next to the church is the former **Turkish Primary School**. Special attention should be paid to the outer doorframe, which is in the Venetian style, whereas the inner doorframe was added later on by the Turks and

The Rimondi Fountain

is ornamented with vines. Thus the initial frame was a much narrower shape. Next to each pilaster pairs of relief work can be seen, which portray lions in the lower part and symbols of the Ottoman Empire in the upper part. The entrance to the school, the lower part of which was built in 1796, is situated in Papamichelaki Street. Continuing along Antistaseos Street, further down you will arrive at **Souliou Street**, which branches to the right. The picturesque alley is worth seeing, since it boasts a large number of shops displaying traditional handicrafts. This street leads up to **Palaiologou St.**, where we turn right. A few metres further down, at the crossroads of Palaiologou and Arkadiou St. the **Loggia** is situated on the right-hand-side. Today, the Ministry

"Porta Guora", The Great Gate

Ethnikis Antistaseos St

◀ *Nerandzes Mosque*

Nikiforos Foka St. (Makry Steno), formerly the central artery of Rethymno, is distinguished by its many doorframes decorated with bas-reliefs.

The door of the Tourkish school

and shops, and turning right into Bernardou St. Here, the **Neratzes mosque** with its towering minaret is situated. The mosque with its impressive dome was the Church of Santa Maria during Venetian times and belonged to the Augustine monastery, which was situated in the centre of the Venetian square. Its imposing doorframe is ornamented with Corinthian capitals and an impressive lintel in the crown of the arch. The Church of Santa Maria was transformed into a mosque in 1657 and the highest minaret of the town furnished with two galleries was added in 1890. **The Folklore Museum of Rethymno** is found at No. 30, Bernardou St, and is worth a visit. Further down the street you can admire one the most beautiful doorframes of Rethymno, which displays the following inscription: "VIRTUTE FULCIDA DOMUS MDCIXKAL JUNII" (Virtue makes this house shine, first days of June 1609). We continue our tour down Bernardou St.

Street scene from Ethnikis Antistaseos St

and arrive at Nikiforos Foka St., at the square of **Kyria ton Aggelon** (Lady of the Angels). The Church of The Little Virgin, as the people of Rethymno call it, was built during the Venetian occupation and dedicated to Maria Magdalene of the Dominican order. During the Turkish occupation, this three-aisled church was transformed into a mosque, and a minaret was added in 1680, which collapsed shortly after. From the square of Kyria ton Aggelon we turn into **Arambatzoglou St.** with its magnificently ornamented facades and doorframes. A

of Culture uses this building as a shop, where authentic copies of ancient artefacts are sold. We turn back in a westerly direction on Palaiologou St. and arrive at the famous **Platanos Square** (Platia Petychaki), where the **Rimondi Fountain**, a remnant of the Venetian period, will be found. It is worthwhile having a closer look at the fountain before continuing through the square with its traditional cafes, tavernas

Traditional grocers on Ethnikis Antistaseos St

The lighthouse of the Venetian port

Rethymnon by night seen from the east

bath was built in 1670 and includes two halls with semi-circular domes. To the west at the crossroads of Radamanthios and Nikiforou Foka St. we turn right and continue down Nikiforos Foka St. We then continue down **Klidis St.,** the first alley on our left-hand-side, which is famous for the superbly ornamented doorframe at **No. 13**. We continue down Klidis St. and then turn left into **Renieri St.** with its beautiful Venetian doorframes and wooden balconies, until we arrive at **Panou Koroneou St.** In this street **No.12** has an exceptionally attractive doorframe with a relief that is richly decorated with natural motifs. Walking down Koroneou St. in a westerly direction you will arrive at the **intersection of Koroneou and Smyrnis St.**, where five fountains can be seen, two on Koroneou St. and three below the arch. Koroneou St. leads us to the square of **Iroon Polytechniou**, which is dominated by the neoclassical building of

large number of wooden balconies, many more than anywhere else in the town, have been preserved in this street. From Arabatzoglou St. we turn into **Mesolongiou St.** and from there we turn left into **Radamanthios St.** The **Turkish bath** was housed at No. 25 during earlier times; but it is now a private building and so it cannot be visited. The

the Prefecture. We return to Koroneou St. and, continuing in an easterly direction, we turn right into **Mavili St**. Here you will notice neatly kept houses with flowers and enclosed yards. We then turn left into **Piga St**., continue down **Patelarou St.** and arrive

The chiselled inscription of Koroneou St. says: "This fountain was built so that the people can drink water. May he who drinks from it and quenches his thirst pray for the soul of the man who built it. 1863."

Continuing along Nikiforos Foka in a southerly direction, we turn left into **Bouniali St.,** where the blacksmiths and saddlers had their workshops in earlier times. Following the road straight on we arrive at **Ethnikis Antistaseos st**. and, looking to the right, we can see the **Great Gate (Porta Guora),** the point from which we started our tour.

at **Nikiforou Foka St.,** the famous Makry Steno (long alley) of the old town of Rethymno. The iconostasis, which is made of stone and built into the wall at this point where Nikiforou Foka St. and Papamichelaki St. meet, is worth seeing.

The Venetian Port

During the Venetian period the mosque Kara Mousa Passa was a monastery dedicated to St. Barbara. The Turks turned into a mosque and also added the minaret, which has been partially preserved up until today. The yard around the temple displays many Turkish gravestones, the so-called "mezaria", which are excellently ornamented in relief. Today the Kara Mousa Passa building houses the preservation workshop of the Trusteeship of Byzantine antiquities

Turkish grave stelae in the courtyard of the Kara Mousa Pasha Mosque

2. The following tour starts at **Ethnarchou Makariou St.,** at house numbers 5, 7, and 9, where we shall see parts of domed buildings, which represented the quarters of the rampart of Aghia Varvara, that is of the first fortification of the town of Rethymno. Following the road further down we arrive at the **square of Iroon,** which has the monument to the Unknown Soldier in its centre. From here we turn into **Arkadiou St.,** one of the most important shopping centres of Rethymno. The **Kara Mousa Pasa mosque** is situated at the corner of Arkadiou and Viktoros Ougo (Victor Hugo) St. We continue down **Arkadiou** and stop at **no. 48** in order to admire the impressive doorframe of this Venetian mansion. Further down we arrive at **no. 154**, Rethymno's most imposing Venetian mansion. It boasts a magnificent facade as well as a distinctive doorframe. Furthermore, **No. 12 Tsouderon St.** also displays a beautiful doorframe with Doric columns, an arch and triangles with curved sides, which are richly ornamented with motifs taken from nature. At the crossroads of Tsouderon and **Tsagri St**. we turn to the right, pass through the vaulted passage and turn right again into Arkadiou St. At this point, that is at the **intersection of Arkadiou and Chatzigrigoraki St.**, you will find an admirable Neoclassical mansion with three storeys. We continue down Arkadiou St. as far as Paleologou St., where the

Arkadiou St

famous **Venetian Loggia** is found on the left hand corner. From there we turn right into **Petychaki St.**, which leads us to the beach promenade of **E. Venizelou.** Following the stone-paved promenade in a westerly direction you will come to the **Venetian port**. Construction works started here in 1300, however they were delayed due to problems of sand being washed up. The wall, which surrounds the port, is also of Venetian origin, whereas some extensions and the lighthouse were built during the Turkish occupation.

Images from the street market ▶

Exploring the Prefecture

- **Rethymno**
- **New National Road**
- **Panormo**
- **Bali**

Moni Atali

Starting from the centre of the town of **Rethymno** take the **New National Road** (either at the intersection of Atsipopoulo to the west, or at Misiria, 3 km east of Rethymno), in the direction of Heraklio. After 9 km on the New National Road Rethymno - Heraklio you arrive at Adelianos Kampos, an area of extensive development of hotel units stretching along the beach. After 21 km from Rethymnon we turn right at the road sign in the direction of the village of Panormo. This coastal village is situated by a beautiful bay, which is inviting for a swim. Worth visiting here are the remains of the Early Christian basilica of Aghia Sofia.

During ancient times **Panormo** acted as the harbour for ancient Eleftherna. Leaving the village we return to the New National Road and follow it in an easterly direction until we come to the 34th km sign at the coastal village of **Bali**

with its clean beaches and its advanced tourism infrastructure. If you turn right 1 km before you arrive at the crossroads to Bali you can visit the excellently restored **Atali Monastery**.

The east beach of Rethymno with its large hotel units

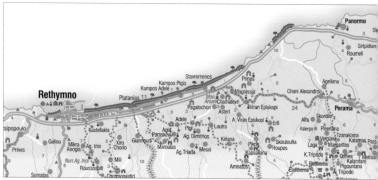

Panormo

Bali

- **Rethymno**
- **Old National Road**
- **Stavromenos**
- **Viran Episkopi**
- **Alexandrou Hani**
- **Perama**
- **Melidoni**
- **Aghios Syllas**
- **Mourtzana**
- **Garazo**
- **Axos**
- **Zoniana**
- **Anoghia**

and the Monastery of Arsani can be visited here. Following the old national road in an easterly direction you will arrive at the village of **Viran Episkopi**, where the remains of a Christian basilica dedicated to Aghios Dimitrios were discovered in 1959. It is presumed that the village represented the See of the Episcopate, which was destroyed during the Arab

The giant bust of the socialist Stavros Kallergis

3 km further on you will arrive at the village of **Perama**, which represents the centre of trade and administration for the wider area of Mylopotamos. After following the provincial road for 4 km you will arrive at the village of **Melidoni**, where the cave of the same name is worth visiting. From there we follow the old national road in the direction of Anoghia, passing through the villages of **Aghios Syllas** and Dafnedes until at the 33rd km marker we reach the village of **Mourzana** with its Venetian buildings and lush vegetation. There

The Aghioi Apostoloi of Axos

The area of **Stavromenos** is located at the 11th km of the Old National Road Rethymno - Heraklio,

occupation and therefore was given the name "Viran", which means destroyed. 8 km to the east is the village of **Alexandrou Hani** and

we turn right and reach **Garazo** after 4 km, which is renowned for its view and its production of citric fruit, and from where we continue in the direction of **Axos**.

After Axos we suggest you continue to the village of **Zoniana**, which is only a short distance off your main route, and visit the cave of Sfendoni.

54 km from your starting point, the town of Rethymno, you will finally arrive at the traditional village of **Anoghia**, situated on the northern foothills of Mount Psiloritis.

A visit to the Ideon Andron is easy to do from here. The cave is located at a height of 1499 m and 22 km away from Anoghia.

Charcoal kiln in the village of Agia

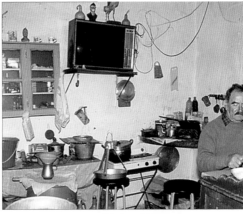

In the village of Anoghia we can relax in one of the traditional cafes (above) and savour the unaltered taste of the Cretan cuisine. Furthermore you will have the opportunity to admire excellent woven cloth, which is nearly produced by the women of Anoghia (down)

- Rethymno
- Platanias
- Adele
- Amnatos
- Kapsaliana
- Arkadi
- Eleftherna
- Ancient Eleftherna
- Margarites
- Hani Alexandrou
- Rethymno

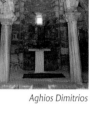

Aghios Dimitrios

The village of **Platanias** is situated on the old National Road, 5 km from Rethymnon, going in the direction of Heraklio. There we turn right at the crossroads to Arkadi. After a few kilometres we come to **Adele**, the home of Kostis Giamboudakis, the hero of the Arkadi holocaust. The village of Adele is the administrative centre of the Municipality of Arkadi. 1 km from Adele the village of Pigi is found. As soon as you have passed Pigi, turn right towards the village of Aghios Dimitrios, where you will find the Byzantine church of the same name. After this brief detour you return to the road leading to Arkadi and at the 18th kilometre you arrive at the village of **Amnatos**, the home of Hariklia Daskalaki, the heroine of the Arkadi holocaust. This village boasts a beautiful view, Venetian buildings and a distinctive doorframe with an inscription.

At a short distance from the village of Amnatos you will arrive at the crossroads to the settlement of **Kapsaliana**, which is also worth visiting. This traditional settlement, which formerly housed the olive press for the Arkadi Monastery, has recently been restored. The Museum of the Olive tree will soon be inaugurated in the village. After having returned to our initial route, and having covered a total distance of 22 km from Rethymno, we

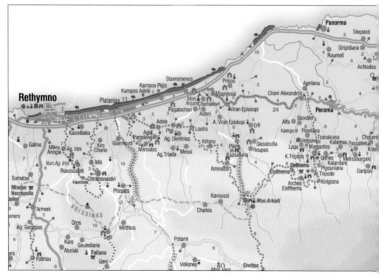

finally arrive at the historical **Arkadi monastery**. From there we continue in the direction of **Eleftherna**, which is situated 7 km from Arkadi and soon after that we arrive at **Ancient Eleftherna**. The village of **Margarites** is found 6 km after Ancient Eleftherna, where the traditional art of pottery is still flourishing. Apart from its beautiful panoramic view this village also boasts Venetian buildings with magnificent doorframes, the Byzantine Churches of Aghios Ioannis the Theologos (14th century with frescoes), of Aghios Georgios (14th century) as well as the bust of the abbot Gabriel Marinakis, who was born in this village and played a leading role in the Arkadi tragedy. From the village of Margarites we return to Rethymno passing through the village of **Alexandrou Chani**.

The castle in Eleftherna

Margarites

The Church of Agios Ioannis of Margarites

- Rethymno
- Aghia Irini
- Roussospiti
- Chromonastiri
- Myli
- Rethymno

Myli

The Church of Panaghia Kera outside the village of Chromonastiri

Leave the centre of the town of **Rethymno** heading in an easterly direction and turn into Theotokopoulou. St. on your right hand side. Follow this road up-hill for about 7 km. After having passed the intersection to the settlement of Mikra

Anoghia, you will arrive at the **Monastery of Aghia Irini**, which has recently been restored and is situated exactly south of the village of the same name. Following the same road for another 2 km, you will come to the village of **Roussospiti**, where the Venetian buildings and the famous fountain are worth visiting. You continue in the direction of **Chromonastiri**. In this area the Churches of Panaghia Kera and Aghios Eftychios can be visited as well as the Venetian mansion 'Villa Clodio'. Taking the road south of Chromonastiri you will arrive at the deserted village of Myli after 1.5 km. In order to visit **Myli** you have to walk down the path, which leads to the gorge, where the village is situated. Its name is derived from the many water mills, which were once in operation. A visit to this

Doorframe in the village of Myli

village is also worthwhile for its abundant vegetation and picturesque location. We return to the asphalt road and continue our tour in the direction of Rethymno. Shortly after the village of Myli you will see the Church of Panaghia Chalevi on your left-hand-side as well as the remains of the monastery of the same name. Following the same road you will finally arrive at Misiria and after 3 km more you will have returned to the centre of **Rethymno**.

The Villa Clodio i[n] Chromonasti[ri]

- Rethymno
- Old National Road
- Prasses
- Potami
- Patsos
- Apostoli
- Syvritos
- Moni Assomaton
- Monastiraki
- Meronas
- Gerakari
- Spili
- Rethymno

Fountain in the village of Spili

Church of Panagia at Meronas with the emblem of the Kallergis family

Starting from the centre of **Rethymno** you follow the **old national road** in the direction of Heraklio. After 3 km, in the area of Mirsiria, turn right at the crossroads in the direction of Amari. 12 km later you will arrive at the village of **Prasses** and 10 km further on at the village of **Potami**, where construction works for the building of a large dam are being carried out. At the village of Potami we suggest you leave the main road and turn in the direction of Bolionies. Continue along this road for 10 km up until you arrive at the village of **Patsos**, where the Kraneo Andro or Cave of Aghios Antonios is worth visiting in the beautiful gorge of Patsos. After that we return to the village of Potami and continue on our main route from the point where we had left it. At a distance of 8 km from that point, the village of **Apostoli** is found, which is built like an amphitheatre. Here we suggest you visit the Church of Aghios Nikolaos (14th century), which is decorated with frescoes. 1 km from there you will arrive at the village of Aghia Fotini, where you turn left in the direction

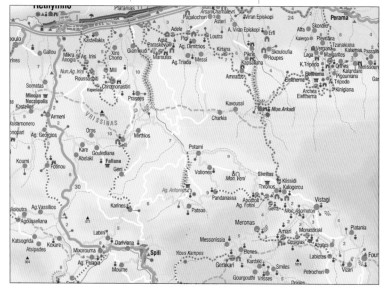

122

The village Nefs Amari in the centre of the Amari valley

Label in the village Potamoi

of the village of Thronos (1 km), the ancient village of **Syvritos**. The village has a panoramic view of the Amari valley and the Church of Panaghia (14th century), which is ornamented with frescoes. Leaving the village of Thronos we continue in the direction of the village of **Moni Asomaton**. During the Byzantine period a magnificent monastery existed in this village, which flourished during the 17th century and was turned into a school of agriculture in 1930. Following a track outside the village we arrive at the Church of Aghia Paraskevi. From the village of Moni Asomaton

we continue in the direction of the village of **Monastiraki** and from there in a westerly direction. After 7 km we arrive at the village of **Meronas** with its rich vegetation and beautiful view. It also boasts remains of Venetian buildings and the Byzantine Church of Panaghia. 5 km from Meronas is the village of **Gerakari**, which is famous for its cultivation of cherries. The village actually nestles among cherry trees and during the blossom time the sight is truly delightful. Following the road in the direction of **Spili** you will easily find the central provincial road, which connects the north and south area of the Prefecture of Rethymno. We suggest you visit the village of Spili and take

a refreshing break at its flowing springs. The distance from Spili back to **Rethymno** is 30 km.

Bridge at Prasses

The entrance to Prasses Gorge

- **Rethymno**
- **Armeni**
- **Fotinou**
- **Mixorrouma**
- **Lampini**
- **Spili - Kissou Kampos**
- **Akoumia**
- **Melampes**
- **Aghia Galini**

Wall painting from the Church of St. Paraskevi in Melambes

Starting from **Rethymno** we follow the central provincial road, which connects the north and the south area of the prefecture of Rethymno. 1 km before we arrive at the first village on our tour, the village of Armeni, we turn right in order to visit the **Late Minoan Cemetery of Armeni**. After having passed through the village of Armeni we suggest you turn right at the road sign in the direction of **Fotinou**. This small

The village of Kato Mixorrouma

village has a famous Venetian fountain dating back to the 17th century. We return to the main road and continue in a southerly direction. After 20 km you will arrive at the crossroads, the right hand branch of which leads to the village of Aghios Vassilios. If you follow this road you will go through the gorge of Kotsifou and finally arrive at the south coast of the prefecture. If you continue on the main road, 2 km later you will see the road sign to the right in the direction of Koxare. This road also leads to the south coast via the famous gorge of Kourtaliotis - to the village of Plakias and to the Monastery of Preveli. Disregarding both intersections we continue in the direction of Spili. 26 km from Rethymno we arrive at the village of **Mixorrouma**, where the traditional art of basket weaving is still alive. If you turn to the left in an easterly direction from Mixorrouma, the road will lead you to the village of **Lampini**, where you may admire the Byzantine Church of Panaghia. Having returned to the main road after 4 km you will arrive at **Spili**, the capital of the Municipality of Lampis. Crystal clear water pours from the fountains at its central square. Leaving Spili behind

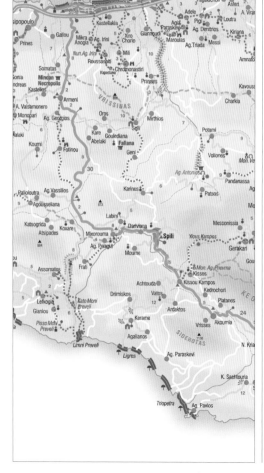

The church of Sotiras Christos in the village of Akoumia

us, we continue on the main road. After having covered a total distance of 35 km from Rethymno you will arrive at the crossroads of **Kissou Kampos**. The road to the right leads to a number of villages such as Adraktos, Drimiskos, Kerame and the beautiful beach Ligres. On the 39th km we arrive to the village of **Akoumia** . The Church of Sotiras is ornamented with frescoes. The road turning to the right inside the village will take you to the famous beach of Akoumia and to the beach of Triopetra .

Agia Galini

The village of Kria Vrissi is situated 54 km from Rethymnon and a little further on you will arrive at the crossroads to Aghios Pavlos

and **Melampes**. You can either follow this road or the central provincial road in order to get to the coastal resort of **Aghia Galini**, which is 58 km from Rethymno.

The mountain of Psiloritis from the village of Melambes

- **Rethymno**
- **Armeni**
- **Koxare**
- **Assomatos**
- **Monastery of Preveli**
- **Lefkoghia**
- **Damnoni**
- **Plakias**
- **Myrthios**
- **Sellia**
- **Rodakino**

Souda

Starting from **Rethymno** in the direction of the village of **Armeni** we follow the main road up as far as the crossroads to **Koxare** (22 km from Rethymno). This road will lead us to the village of **Assomatos** via the gorge of Kouraliotis. From Assomatos we proceed south following the road sign on the left in the direction of the **Monastery of Preveli** and the village of **Lefkoghia**. After 2 km you can either take the road to the left in order to visit the monastery, or continue to the right in the direction of the village of Lefkoghia. Having left Lefkoghia behind you will have the opportunity to visit the magnificent beaches

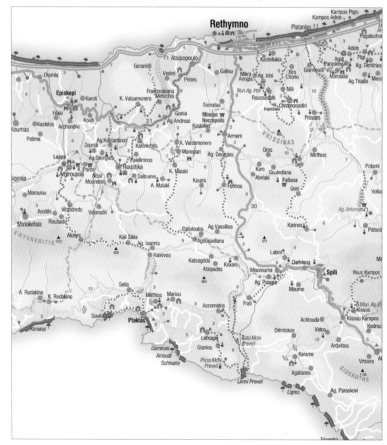

The village of Plakias ▶

Iconostasis at Rodakino

Preveli Monastery

The beach of Preveli

of Skinaria, **Damnoni**, Ammoudi and **Plakias**. From Plakias the road leads up-hill to the village of **Myrthios**, which is situated 4km north of Plakias and offers a superb view of the bay of Plakias and the Libyan Sea. We continue in the direction of the gorge of Kotsifou. Shortly before reaching the narrow part of the gorge we turn to the right in the direction of the village of **Sellia**, which is situated at a height of 280 m and also offers an excellent view of the Libyan Sea. Approximately 12 km west of Sellia is the village of **Rodakino**, with its marvellous beach of Korakas south of the village. Although the road to Rodakino is very twisty you will enjoy the magnificent landscape.

After Rodakino

The Byzantine Church of Aghioi Assomatoi at the village of Assomatos

Arum cre

- **Rethymno**
- **Atsipopoulo**
- **Aghios Andreas**
- **Ano Valsamonero**
- **Monopari**
- **Roustika**
- **Aghios Konstantinos**
- **Argyroupoli**
- **Episkopi**

Starting our tour from **Rethymno** we continue in a westerly direction on the old national road towards Chania. 6 km later we arrive at the picturesque village of **Atsipopoulo** with its beautiful Venetian buildings. Passing through the villages of Prines and Gonia we come to the village of **Aghios Andreas**.

There we turn left and after 3 km the village of **Ano Valsamonero** lies ahead of you. Outside the village you can visit the fortress of **Monopari**, which was built by Pescatore on the precipitous hill of Kastellos. We return to Aghios Andreas and continue south. After 2 km we follow the road sign to the village of **Roustika**, which is situated 21 km from Rethymno. We suggest you visit the Monastery of Profitis Elias as well as the beautiful two-aisled church, which is ornamented with frescoes and dedicated to the Assumption of the Virgin and the Metamorphosis of Christ. We leave Roustika and continue in the direction of **Aghios Konstantinos**. This village has magnificent Venetian buildings and used to be the resort of the Venetian nobility. Passing through a number of smaller villages we arrive at **Argyroupoli** with its many springs of crystal clear water and the remains of the ancient city of **Lappa**. The village of Myriokefala is situated 7 km south of Argyroupoli, where we suggest you visit the Monastery of the Virgin, which dates back to the 10th century. We then return to Argyroupoli and continue north until we arrive 5 km later at the village of **Episkopi**, the capital of the newly established Lappeon Municipality.

We go on in a northerly direction until we arrive at the New National Road Rethymno - Chania, where we may turn in either direction.

View from Monopari

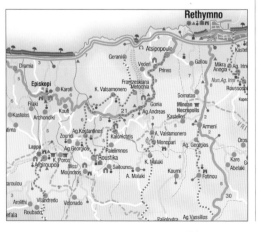

130

Argyroupoli

The springs of Argyroupoli

Street in Argyroupoli

Roman inscription built into a door frame at Arygroupoli

Agios Konstantinos

Foot & bike routes

The multifarious morphology of the landscape in the area of Rethymno including a plethora of mountain peaks, gorges, plateaux

and beaches allows for a variety of contact with nature. It offers alternatives from simple walking tours and passing through gorges to experienced mountain climbing and difficult excursions involving mountaineering. Apart from the well-signed

walking path E4, there are a variety of smaller or larger excursions some of which are described herein. Most of the less difficult walking tours offer the opportunity to the visitor to discover the surrounding landscape of the village where he is staying. Thus he will experience the genuine Crete, he will make friends and enrich his holiday with impressions and pictures that do not exist in any tourist brochure. However, Rethymno not only represents a paradise for walkers but also for cyclists. Beautiful country roads with little traffic are particularly suitable for bicycle tours, while most of the tracks in the countryside make ideal routes for mountain

The gorge of Patsos

biking. So, do not hesitate to experience the nature of Crete as well as its hospitable people.

The Cretan countryside is a paradise for those in search of rare flora

RETHYMNO - VRISINAS 8H

Roussospiti - Kapediana - Vrisinas - Chromonastiri - Mili - Perivolia

ADELE - AG. PARASKEVI - MAROULAS - PLATANES 2H

ATSIPOPOULO - GERANI

Atsipopoulo - Prines - Gonia - Kalonichtis - Roustika - Ag. Konstantinos - K. Varsamonero - Metochia - Gerani

RETHYMNO - ARKADI

Rethymno - Viran Episkopi - Margarites - Eleftherna - Arkadi - Kyrianna - Adele - Platanes

PRASANO FARAGI 4H

FARAGI PATSOU 2H

ARKADI - PIKRIS 2H

ASSOMATOS - LEFKOGIA 6H

Assomatos -Kato Moni Preveli - Limni Preveli -Piso Moni Preveli - Gianiou - Lefkogia

GIROS PLAKIA 3H

Plakias - Selia - Finikas - Souda - Plakias

ANO VALSAMONERO - AGOUSELIANA 5.30H

Ano Valsamonero - Monopari (Castle 45′) - Kato Malaki - Nifis Potamia - Agouseliana

ARKADI - THRONOS 2.30H

DOXARO - MONI VOSSAKOU - SISSES 3.30H

ANO MEROS - KEDROS 4.30H

Ano Meros - Moni Kaloidenas - Tripiti - Kedros

FRATI - KATO MIXOROUMA 1.15H

ARMENI - FOTINOU - BALE 2.15H

SELI - GENI - KARINES 2H

MOUNTROS - VELONADO 2H

MOUNTROS - NISSI - KATO POROS 2H

▪ **ARGIROUPOLI - AG. IOANNIS** 4H

Argyroupoli - Vilandredo - Alones - Kali Sikia - Ag. Ioannis

GERAKARI - KISSOU KAMBOS 2H

MERONAS - VIZARI 2.30H

Meronas - Amari - Opsigias - Monastiraki - Labiotes - Vizari

PANTANASSA - SCHOLI ASSOMATON 2.30H

Pantanassa - Apostoli - Ag. Fotini - Gena - Scholi Assomaton

On the E4 Path

On the path to Psiloritis

The European path of long distance- walking E4 starts in the Pyrenean Mountains, crosses through the Alps and Yugoslavia and - arriving at Florina - continues on Greek territory. Starting from the town of Florina the E4 continues through the Greek mainland up until the town of Gythio, and from there - imaginary - across the sea to the village of Kastelli/ Kissamos on Crete. It leads across the island and ends at Zakros. In Rethymno the path is divided into two sections, one coming from Argyroupoli in the north and the other one coming from Rodakino in the south of the island. Both routes cover the entire prefecture displaying an ever-changing landscape of particular beauty until they finally merge on the Nida plateau. From there the path continues through the prefecture of Heraklio. The path E4 gives the walker the opportunity to experience the unknown nature of the island, the old village paths, the traditional settlements and the monasteries as well as the high mountains of Crete.

Amari. On the road to Fourfouras

SOUTH PART

ARGYROUPOLI - ANGOUSELIANA, 23 KM, 7 - 8 H,
🚶💺🔃⛽⚙

Argyroupoli - Kato Poros - 2.5 km south - 1 km east - north in the direction of Moundros - south through the gorge of Moundros - east - southeast up until the village of Angouseliana.

ANGOUSELIANA - SPILI, 13.3 KM, 4 H
🚶🔃⛽⚙

Angouseliana - southeast in the direction of Koxare - Aghia Pelagia - Ano Mixorrouma, Spili.

SPILI - GERAKARI, 18.5 KM, 8 H
🚶💺✧⛽🔻⚙

Follow the road from Spili in the direction of Kissos. Turn in a southeasterly direction after approximately 1 km from the village and near the monastery; then turn east towards the peak of Mount Kedros (1776 m) and follow the road to Gerakari

GERAKARI - FOURFOURAS - REFUGE, 22 KM 5+3,5-4 H
🚶💺〰⛽🔻⚙🅰

From Gerakari in the direction of the villages Elenes, Amari, Opsigias, Lampiotes, Vyzari, Fourfouras. From Fourfouras follow the road sign to the organised Refuge of "Toumpotos Prinos" which is situated at a height of 1400 m on the southern slopes of Mount Psiloritis. For the use of the refuge please contact the EOS (Greek Mountain Climbing Society) of Rethymno beforehand.

TIMIOS STAVROS - NIDA, 3.5 + 2.5 H
🚶🄵💺✧🔻⚙🅰

Rocky and precipitous track to Timios Stavros, the peak of Psiloritis, (2,454 m). Waterless and barren area. A magnificent view of the entire island from the peak. From there follow the clearly signed path to the Nida plateau.

NORTH PART

RODAKINO - AGHIOS KONSTANTINOS, 20.5 KM., 7-8
🚶💺⛽⚙

Starting from Kato Rodakino and continuing in a northerly direction you will arrive at the village Aghios Konstantinos

AGHIOS KONSTANTINOS - ARMENI 15 KM, 5 H
🚶💺🔃⛽⚙

From Aghios Konstantinos turn east in the direction of Kalonychti, Ano Valsamonero, Armeni.

ARMENI - ARKADI, 29 KM, 9 - 10 H
🚶💺〰⛽🔻🅰⚙

Follow the road from Armeni to Mount Brysina and continue on field tracks to the villages of Selli, Prasses, Harkia, Kavousi, and Arkadi.

ARKADI - GARAZO, 32 KM, 11 - 12 H
🚶💺〰⛽🔻⚙

Starting from Arakadi you pass the villages of Eleftherna, Kato Tripodo, Margarites, Orthes, Kalandares, Kalamas, Passalites, Houmeri, Dafnedes, Episkopi, Garazo.

GARAZO - ANOGHIA, 16 KM, 5 H
🚶💺⛽⚙

From Garazo to the Diskouriou Monastery, Zoniana and from there continue on the asphalt road in the direction of Anoghia.

ANOGHIA - ZOMINTHOS - NIDA, 11 + 11 KM, 7 H
🚶💺〰🔻⚙

From Anoghia to Zominthos and then in the direction of the Nida plateau, from where a path will lead you to the villages of Zaros and Kamares.

INDEX

A

Adele, 16, 118
Aghia, 117
Aghia Dynami, 30
Aghia Galini, **32**, 84, 125
Aghia Irini, Monastery, **69**, 120
Aghia Paraskevi, Panagia church, 64
Aghios Andreas, 130
Aghios Frangiskos, 81, 108
Aghios Konstandinos, 130
Aghios Pavlos, **32**
Aghios Syllas, 117
Akoumia, 32, 124
Akoumia, Sotiras Christos church, 64
Alexandrou Chani, 116
Amaltheia, 37, 59
Ammoudi, **32**
Amnatos, 118
Ancient Eleftherna, Sotiras Christos church, 63
Anogheia, 102, 117
Apodoulou, 38, 57, 84
Apodoulou, Aghios Georgios Xififoros church, 65
Apollon, 40
Apostoloi, 122
Arabatzoglou, street, 109
Argyroupoli, 17, **30**, 55, 84, 130
Ariadne, 36
Arkadi, Monastery, 66
Arkadiotiko, gorge, 24, **26**
Arkadiou, street, 112
Arkas, 89
Armenoi, 38, 84, 124, 126
Armenoi, LM cemetery, 54
Assomatoi, Aghia Paraskevi church, 65
Atalis / Bali, Monastery, **69**, 114
Athena, 40
Atsipopoulo, 130
Avlopotamos, 11
Axos, 38, **56**, 117, 84
Axos, Aghia Irini church, **62**

B

Bali, 31, 114
Barbarossa Hairedin, 42
Baxevanis, 100
Bonifatius of Montferrato, 41
Bouniali, street, 111
Bounialis Emm'., 43
Bounialis Marinos Tzanes, 43

C

Chalevi, Monastery, 70, 120
Chamalevri, 38
Chania, 7, 11
Chromonastiri, villa clodio, **83**, 120
Churches
Aghia Anna, Nefs Amari, **65**

Aghia Irini, Axos, **62**
Aghia Paraskevi, Assomati, **65**
Aghia Paraskevi, Melampes, **64**
Aghios Dimitrios, Viran Episkopi, **63**
Aghios Georgios Xififoros, Apodoulou, **65**
Aghios Georgios, Kalamas, **62**
Aghios Georgios, Mourne, **64**
Aghios Georgios, Opsogias, **64**
Aghios Ioannis, Episkopi Mylopotamou, **62**
Aghios Ioannis, Margarites, **63**
Aghios Ioannis, Margarites. **64**
Agios Eftychios, Chromonastiri, **63**
Kimisi Theotokou, Drymiskos, **64**
Kimisi Theotokou, Lambini, **63**
Kimisi Theotokou, Thronos, **65**
Metamorphosi Sotira, Myrthios, **63**
Panaghia Kera, Nefs Amari, **64**
Panaghia, Aghia Paraskevi, **64**
Panaghia, Meronas, **65**
Panaghia, Prinos, **63**
Sotiras Christos, Akoumia, **64**
Sotiras Christos, Ancient Eleftherna, **63**
Claudius Aelianos, 40
Claudius Potlemaeus, 40
Clodio, villa, **83**

D

Dafnedes, 117
Damnoni, **31**, 126
Deukalion, 36
Dikti, 7
Diktynna, 36
Diskouriou, Monastery, 70
Drymiskos, Koimisi Theotokou church, 64

E

Eleftehrna, 38, **52**, 84, 118
Eleftherna, early christian basilica, **62**
Elenes, cave, 38
Episkopi, **31**, 130
Episkopi (Mylopotamos), Aghios Ioannis church, **62**
Ethnarhou Makariou, street, 112
Ethnikis Antistasseos, street, 111
Europa, 36

F

Fandaxospiliara Prinou, cave, 38
Finikas, beach, 29
Fokas Nikiforos, 41
Fortezza of Rethymnon, **74**
Foteinou, 124
Foustalieris Stelios, 100
Franzeskakis, collection, 87

G

Garazo, 117

Gavriil Marinakis, 119
Gerani, cave, 20, **22**, 38, 84
Geropotamos, 11
Giamboudakis Kostis, 66
Giannoudi, 39
Goulediana, early christian basilica, **62**

H

Hantzopoulos Dimitris, 89
Herakleion, 7, 11
Hermes Kraneos, 22
Hortatzis Georgios, 43, 65
Hussein Pasha, 46

I

Ida, 7, 11, 12
Idaion Andron 20, 38, **59**, 117
Iroon Polytechniou, square, 110

K

Kalamas, Aghios Georgios church, 63
Kallergis Alexios, 65
Kalliergis Zaharias, 42, 43
Kaloidenas, Monastery, 71
Kalokyris, 40
Kanakakis, gallery, 86
Kaounis Emm., 58
Kapsaliana, 16
Kara Mousa Passa, mosque, 112
Katsivelos, Eleftherna, **53**
Kissos, Aghios Ioannis church, **64**, 124
Kleidi, street, 110
Korakas, **32**
Koroneou, street, 110
Kotsyfou, gorge, **24**, 128
Kouloukounas, 11
Kourites, 37, 59
Kourtaliotis, gorge, **24**
Koxare, 24, 126
Kronos, 36
Krya Vryssi, 32, 125
Kryoneritis, 11

L

Labini, Kimisi Theotokou church, 63, 124
Lagos Manolis, 100
Lambardos Emm., 43
Lappa, 30, 38, **55**, 130
Lasithi, 7
Lefkogeia, 126
Livadia, 102
Loggia, **82**, 108

M

Makry Steno (Long Alley), 111
Maragrites, 101, 119
Margarites, Aghios Ioannis church, 63

Mastabas, 40, 84
Mavili, street, 111
Mechmet Ali, 47
Melabes, Aghia Paraskevi, **64**, 125
Melidon, cave, **20**, 38, 84
Melidoni, 116
Melissinou, street, 51
Minos, 36
Minotaurus, 36
Mixorouma, 124
Monasteries, 66
Moni Aghias Irinis, 69
Moni Antifonitrias, Myriokefala, 71
Moni Arkadiou, 66
Moni Arsaniou, 68
Moni Atalis / Bali, 69
Moni Chalevi, 70
Moni Diskouriou, 70
Moni Kaloidenas, 71
Moni Preveli, 68
Moni Prophet Elias, 71
Moni Vossakou, 70
Monastiraki, 38, **57**, 84, 123
Monopari, fortress, **79**, 130
Moundakis Kostas, 98
Moundros, mansion, **83**
Moungri, cave, 20
Mourne, Aghios Georgios church, **64**
Mourtzana, 117
Mousouros Markos, 43
Myli, gorge, 24, 120
Mylopotamos, 11
Myriokefala, Monastery, 71
Myrthios, 128
Myrthios, Metamorphosi Sotira church, 63

N

Nefs Amari, Aghia Anna church, 65
Nefs Amari, Panagia church, 64
Neratzes, mosque, **81**, 109
Nida, plateau, 20, **30**, 59
Nikiforoou Foka, street, 109

O

Oaxos, **56**
Onyhthe, 38
Opsigias, Aghios Georgios church, 64
Orthi Petra, Eleftherna, **53**

P

Pagalochori,, 38, 58
Paleokastro, 40
Paleologou, street, 108
Panormo, 11, **31**, 114
Panormo, early christian basilica, **62**
Pasiphae, 36
Patelarou, street, **111**
Patsos, 122

Patsos, cave, 20, **22**, 38
Patsos, gorge, 24, **26**
Pente Parthenes (Five Virgins), 30, 55
Pera Galinoi, 38
Perama, 116
Pescatore Enrico, 41, 79
Petychaki, square, 109
Piga, street, 111
Plakias, **31**, 126
Platanias, 118
Platanos, square, 109
Plinius, 40
Potamoi, 122
Prasses, 122
Prasses, gorge, 24, **26**
Preveli, lake, 11, 12, 14, 24, **29**, **32**
Preveli, Monastery, **68**, 126
Prinos, Panagia church, 63
Prophet Elias, Monastery, 71
Psilorits, 7, 11, 12
Pyrgi, Eleftherna, **53**

R

Radamanthios, street, 110
Radamanthys, 36
Rea, 36
Renieri, street, 110
Rimondi, fountain, **81**, 109
Rithymna, 38, **40**
Rodakino, 32, 128
Rodinos Andreas, 100
Rokkaia Artemis, 40
Roussospiti, 120
Roussospiti, fountain, **81**

S

S(f)endoni, cave, **22**, 38
Sarpenon, 36
Sfakaki, 58
Simonelli, cave, 20
Skordalos Thanasis, 100
Smyrnis, street, 110
Souda Plakias, **31**
Souliou, street, 108
Spili, 123
Stagakis Manolis, 100
Stathis, 89
Stavromeno, **58**, 116
Syvritos, 38, **56**, 123

T

Talaea Mountains, 11, 36
Talos, 36
Theodor de Hiostak, 50
Thronos, early christian basilica, **62**
Thronos, Kimisi Theotokou church, **65**
Triopetra, **32**
Troilos, 43

Tsagri, street, 112
Tsouderon, street, 112
Turkish Primary School, 108

U

Ulutz Ali, 42

V

Valsamonero, 130
Vederoi, gorge, 24
Vergikioi, 43
Vergikios Angelos, 37
Viran Episkopi
Viran Episkopi, Aghios Dimitrios church, 63
Vlastos Nikolaos, 43
Vossakos, Monastery, 70
Vritomartis, 36
Vrysinas, 11, 38, 84
Vyzari, early christian basilica, **62**

W

White Mountains (Lefka ori), 12

Y

Yus Kambos, plain, 14

Z

Zeus, 36, 59
Zominthos, 38
Zoniana, 102, 117
Zoniana, S(f)endoni cave, **22**, 38